Michel de Montaigne

Apology for
Raymond Sebond

Translated by
Roger Ariew and Marjorie Grene

Hackett Publishing Company, Inc.
Indianapolis/Cambridge

08 07 06 05 04 03   1 2 3 4 5 6 7

For further information, please address:

Hackett Publishing Company, Inc.
P.O. Box 44937
Indianapolis, IN   46244-0937

www.hackettpublishing.com

Cover design by Listenberger Design & Associates
Interior design by Meera Dash
Composition by William Hartman
Printed at Edwards Brothers, Inc.

Library of Congress Cataloging-in-Publication Data

Montaigne, Michel de, 1533–1592.
  [Apologie de Raymond Sebond, English]
  Apology for Raymond Sebond / Michel de Montaigne; translated
by Roger Ariew and Marjorie Grene.
    p. cm.
  Includes bibliographical references.
  ISBN 0-87220-680-7 — ISBN 0-87220-679-3 (pbk.)
  1. Raymond, of Sabunde, d. 1436.   I. Ariew, Roger.
II. Grene, Marjorie Glicksman, 1910– .   III. Title.

PQ1642.E7A66 2003
844'.3 — dc21
                                        2003042347

Contents

Introduction

1. Montaigne: Life and Times

Michel de Montaigne was born in 1533 at the chateau de Montaigne (about 30 miles east of Bordeaux), the son of Pierre Eyquem, Seigneur de Montaigne, and Antoinette de Louppes (or Lopez), who came from a wealthy (originally Iberian) Jewish family. The many Montaigne children were raised as Catholics, although, unlike Michel, some of them became Protestants. Because of his father's unusual educational ideas, from the age of two to six Michel was taught Latin by a German private tutor who knew no French; thus he learned that language as if it were his native tongue. In 1539 or 1540 Michel de Montaigne entered the Collège de Guyenne at Bordeaux; he dazzled his teachers with his knowledge of Latin, but the experience left him mostly unpleasant memories of the harshness of their pedagogical methods. In 1554, when Pierre Eyquem was elected Mayor of Bordeaux, Montaigne, aged twenty-one, was named counselor to the Cour des Aides at Périgueux, a position newly created by Henry II to assist with tax cases. The Cour was abolished three years later, but it was incorporated into the Parlement of Bordeaux. Thus, in 1557 Montaigne became counselor to the Parlement of Bordeaux, a position he kept until 1570.

During these years Montaigne developed a close friendship with his colleague at the Parlement, the Stoic Etienne de La Boétie; the friendship began in 1557 and ended with La Boétie's death in 1563. Montaigne married Françoise de la Chassaigne in 1565. The marriage produced six daughters over the next eighteen years, but only Léonor, the second daughter, born in 1571, lived beyond infancy. Montaigne's father died in 1568; Pierre Eyquem's property was divided among his five sons and three daughters with some provisions being made for his widow and with Montaigne inheriting the estate and the title Seigneur de Montaigne. In 1569 he published his translation of Raymond Sebond's *Natural Theology* (2nd revised edition, 1581), which he had undertaken at the request of Pierre Eyquem, "the best father who ever was." Then in 1570 Montaigne sold his position as counselor in Bordeaux, went to Paris to publish the Latin poems of La Boétie with their French translations and a companion volume of La Boétie's French poetry, and then retired to his estates. Montaigne commemorated his retirement with the following inscription in his library:

In the year of Christ 1571, at the age of thirty-eight, on the eve of the first of March, his birthday, Michel de Montaigne, already long weary of his servitude to the Parlement and to his public duties, still in full vigor, retired to the bosom of the learned virgins where, in rest and security, he will spend the remaining days of his life. May destiny allow him to complete this home, the sweet retreat of his ancestors, which he has consecrated to his liberty, tranquillity, and leisure!

However, Montaigne's plans for a quiet retreat did not work out: civil war and diplomatic affairs interfered. In 1571 he was made knight of the order of Saint Michael and gentleman ordinary of the king's chamber. But this was also the period during which Montaigne started the *Essays* (with Part I dating from 1572–4) and read Plutarch assiduously (1572 being the year of the publication of Jacques Amyot's translation of *Oeuvres morales*). Montaigne began his examination of Sextus Empiricus' *Hypotyposes* in 1575–6; to commemorate the occasion in 1576 he had a medal struck with his coat of arms and the insignia of Saint Michael on one side and, on the other, the image of a balance, that is, a pair of scales, with the inscription "What do I know?" The same year, Montaigne started writing the *Apology for Raymond Sebond*, which he initially published with the first two books of his *Essays* in Bordeaux in 1580 (2nd edition, 1582). While he was on an extended tour of Italy, he was elected Mayor of Bordeaux, a position he held for two consecutive two-year terms (1582–6), followed by permanent retirement.

The main events of Montaigne's second retirement were the beginnings of his friendship in 1586 with Pierre Charron, whose treatise, *De la Sagesse* (1601; 2nd revised edition, 1604), constituted a powerful echo of Montaigne's *Apology*, and in 1588, his visit to Marie de Gournay, whom he regarded as a second daughter. In 1588 Montaigne published his third book of *Essays*, in Paris, together with many additions to the first two books. He died peacefully in 1592 during a mass that was being recited in his room. In 1595, de Gournay, who became his literary executrix, published in Paris the "Bordeaux copy" of the *Essays*, containing his final revisions to the 1588 edition. The *Essays* were soon translated into English (1613) and Italian (1633); they significantly influenced numerous thinkers in subsequent generations, not the least among them being René Descartes and Blaise Pascal.

2. The *Apology*

In two major moves, the *Apology* puts forward the thesis that the only proper attitude for a Christian is squarely based on faith, not reason. First, if it is objected to Sebond that he should not be presenting arguments in support of Christianity, it is conceded that these must always be based on the prior acceptance of revelation; if revelation comes first, reason may have a secondary, merely ancillary, place. As it is, Montaigne remarks, our acceptance of religion is merely conventional; we need to turn back to living faith as the true source of our beliefs.

Second, if objections are raised to Sebond's arguments themselves, these objections again support the priority of faith, since nothing our reason produces is of much use in any case. Montaigne now proceeds to undermine any claims people may make to any special knowledge, drawing in part from the tropes of Sextus Empiricus, whom he had recently been reading. His first, idiosyncratic, argument is a long comparison of humans and beasts, in which he shows the superiority of the latter, whose behavior is purely natural and without the foolish pretensions we make of being gifted with some peculiar insights. Such claims are illusory; it is ignorance and obedience, not some alleged wisdom, which leads us to God.

In harmony with this position, Montaigne finds radical skepticism, of the Pyrrhonian variety, the only proper intellectual attitude. Consider the endless conflicts among philosophical dogmatists: each school sets up its own allegedly indisputable first principles, in contradiction to those of every other sect. But there are no first principles for us unless God has revealed them. Consider the alternative: dogmatists cannot prove that we really experience what we seem to experience; nor, on the other side, can they tell us what that rational faculty is that is supposed to guide us. Our only basis for understanding ourselves, again, is revelation.

In contrast to the Pyrrhonians, the Academic skeptics consider some judgments more probable than others. But that is nonsense, for our judgments are exceedingly unstable, changing with every change in ourselves, whether physical or emotional. All we can do, as the Pyrrhonians suggest, is to follow the customs of our country, making no claim to know better. The history of the sciences gives the same message: Copernicus proposes to replace Ptolemy; who knows what will happen in another thousand years. The variety in ethical and religious customs further supports radical skepticism.

Finally, a thoroughgoing critique of the "knowledge" gained through our senses undermines any claims we might have to any knowledge whatsoever. All our seeming knowledge arises from our five senses. But, first, how do we know there are not other senses that we lack? Further, the senses we do have constantly deceive us. There are illusions of sense, false opinions induced by passion, dreams very like waking appearances and vice versa. Our senses, again, differ from those of animals; maybe they have access to reality that we lack. Besides, people's sensations differ not only in varied circumstances but also from those of other individuals. Ultimately we face the problem of the criterion: if we try to establish some standard of judgment, that standard in turn demands another standard, and so on ad infinitum. Thus we are thrown back to sense, which guarantees nothing about its apparent objects. Only through the grace of God, in humility and obedience, can we escape our unhappy situation.

3. Notes on the Text

There are three main strata to the text of the *Essays*, and thus to the *Apology*. These are usually referred to as A, B, and C: the text as published before 1588, that is, from the editions of 1580 and 1582; materials Montaigne added in the edition of 1588 (which we are indicating by < >); and those he added after 1588 (which we are indicating by << >>), as represented in the posthumous edition of 1595.

Passages in italics signify that Montaigne quoted the passage in its original language, usually Latin, but sometimes Greek or Italian.

We have tried to keep the structure of Montaigne's sentences and paragraphs, even that of some of his very long sentences, in part to convey the rhythm of Montaigne's discourse. But we have broken up the lengthy, uninterrupted *Apology* by introducing some (bracketed) titles and subtitles.

4. Selected Bibliography of Primary and Secondary Sources

Bencivenga, Ermanno. *The Discipline of Subjectivity: An Essay on Montaigne* (Princeton: Princeton University Press, 1990).

Berven, Dikka. *Montaigne: A Collection of Essays: A Five Volume Anthology of Scholarly Articles* (New York: Garland, 1995).

Brunschvicg, Léon. *Descartes et Pascal, Lecteurs de Montaigne* (Neuchâtel: Editions de la Baconnière, 1945).

Brush, Craig B. *Montaigne and Bayle. Variations on the Theme of Skepticism* (The Hague: Nijhoff, 1966).

Faye, Emmanuel. *Philosophie et Perfection de l'Homme* (Paris: Vrin, 1998).

Floridi, Luciano. *Sextus Empiricus: The Transmission and Recovery of Pyrrhonism* (Oxford: Oxford University Press, 2002).

Frame, Donald. *Montaigne: A Biography* (New York: Harcourt, 1965).

Friedrich, Hugo. *Montaigne*, trans. P. Desan (Berkeley: University of California Press, 1991).

Hartle, Ann. *Michel de Montaigne: Accidental Philosopher* (Cambridge: Cambridge University Press, 2003).

Hoffmann, George. *Montaigne's Career* (Oxford: Clarendon Press, 1999).

Montaigne, Michel de. *Oeuvres complètes*, ed. A. Thibaudet and M. Rat (Paris: Gallimard, 1962).

———. *Complete Essays of Montaigne*, trans. D. Frame (Palo Alto: Stanford University Press, 1965).

———. *The Complete Essays*, trans. M. A. Screech (New York: Penguin, 1991).

O'Neill, John. *Essaying Montaigne: A Study of the Renaissance Institution of Writing and Reading* (London: Routledge, 1982).

Popkin, Richard H. *The History of Scepticism from Savonarola to Bayle* (Oxford: Oxford University Press, 2003).

Quint, David. *Montaigne and the Quality of Mercy: Ethical and Political Themes in the "Essais"* (Princeton: Princeton University Press, 1998).

Rendall, Steven. *Distinguo: Reading Montaigne Differently* (Oxford: Oxford University Press, 1992).

Schaefer, David Lewis. *The Political Philosophy of Montaigne* (Ithaca: Cornell University Press, 1990).

Screech, M. A. *Montaigne and Melancholy* (London: Duckworth, 1983).

Starobinski, Jean. *Montaigne in Motion*, trans. A. Goldhammer (Chicago: University of Chicago Press, 1985).

Supple, James J. *Arms versus Letters: The Military and Literary Ideals in the "Essais" of Montaigne* (Oxford: Oxford University Press, 1984).

Villey, Pierre. *Les sources et l'évolution des Essais de Montaigne*, 2 vols. (2nd ed. Paris: Hachette, 1933).

Apology for Raymond Sebond

Knowledge is indeed a very useful and great accomplishment. Those who despise it give evidence enough of their own stupidity. Yet, all the same, I do not rate its value as extremely as do some, like Herillus the philosopher, who made it the supreme good, and held that knowledge had the power to make us wise and contented.[1] This I do not believe, nor what others have said, that science is the mother of all virtue and that all vice is produced by ignorance. If this is true, it needs a lengthy commentary.

[1. Sebond and His Treatise]

My house has long been open to the learned and is well-known to them. My father, who governed it for more than fifty years, was inflamed with the new ardor with which Francis the First embraced letters and brought them into favor. He sought with great care and expense the acquaintance of the learned, welcoming them to his house like sacred persons who had some special inspiration from divine wisdom. He received their pronouncements and their discourse like oracles, with all the more reverence and religion as he was less able to judge of them. For he had no knowledge of letters, any more than his predecessors. As for me, I like letters well enough, but I do not worship them.

One of these was Pierre Bunel,[2] a man with a great reputation for learning in his time. After staying a few days at Montaigne in the company of my father and others of his sort, on leaving Bunel made him a present of a book called *The Natural Theology of Raymond Sebond*.[3] Since the Italian and Spanish languages were familiar to my father, and the book was constructed from a Spanish rigged up with Latin endings, Bunel hoped that with just a little help my father would derive benefit from it. So he recommended it to him as a very useful book, appropriate to the period in which he gave it to him. This was when the novelties of

---

1. Diogenes Laertius, *Lives of the Philosophers*, VII, 165; Cicero, *Academics*, II, xlii and *De finibus*, II, xiii.

2. Pierre Bunel (1499–1546) was a humanist from Toulouse.

3. *Theologia naturalis sive liber creaturum magistri Raymondi de Sabunde* (1487).

Luther were beginning to gain favor and to shake our traditional belief in many places.

He showed very good judgment, predicting, on the basis of sound reasoning, that this onset of illness would easily degenerate into abominable atheism. For the common people, unable to judge things for themselves, let themselves be carried away by chance and by appearances once they have been given the temerity to despise and contradict the opinions they had held in extreme reverence, such as those that have to do with their salvation. When articles of their religion have been brought into doubt and left in the balance, they soon cast into equal uncertainty all the other items of their belief, for these had no greater authority or foundation among them than those just questioned, and they shake off like a yoke all the impressions they had received from the authority of the law or reverence for long usage:

<For once too much dreaded, now it is easily trampled.>[4]

From then on they are determined to receive nothing to which they have not applied their own judgment and given their specific consent.

Now, a few days before his death, my father happened upon this book beneath a heap of other abandoned papers and asked me to translate it for him into French. It is pleasant to translate authors like this one, where there is only the subject matter to be represented, but those who have given much to grace and elegance of language are risky to undertake, <<especially when transferring them to a weaker medium.>> It was a very strange and new occupation for me, but since I happened to be at leisure and could not refuse a request from the best father who ever was, I got through it as well as I could. He took a singular pleasure from the translation and ordered that it be published; this was done after his death.

I found the author's ideas fine, the texture of his work well-crafted, and his project full of piety. Since many people take pleasure in reading him—and especially the ladies, to whom we have to give particular assistance—I have often been able to help them by defending the book against the two principal objections that are made to it. Its aim is bold and courageous, for Sebond undertakes through natural, human arguments to establish and confirm all the articles of the Christian religion against the atheists. In this, to tell the truth, I find him so firm and so solicitous that I do not think it would be possible to do better in that argument, and I believe no one has equaled him.

4. Lucretius, *De rerum natura*, V, 1139.

Since this work seemed to me too rich and too fine for an author whose name is little known and of whom we know only that he was Spanish and that he practiced medicine at Toulouse about two hundred years ago, I once inquired of Adrianus Turnebus,[5] who knew everything, what could be said about that book. He replied that he thought it a distillation derived from Saint Thomas Aquinas: for, indeed, only that mind, full of infinite erudition and of admirable subtlety, would be capable of such thoughts. Be that as it may, whoever is the book's author and inventor (and without greater cause it is unreasonable to deprive Sebond of that title), he was a very talented man with many fine qualities.

[2. First Objection against Sebond, and Montaigne's Reply]

The first objection made to his work is that Christians are wrong in wanting to base their belief on human arguments, a belief that is conceivable only through faith and by a particular inspiration of divine grace. In this objection it seems that there is some pious zeal; and for that reason we must try, with as much mildness and respect as possible, to answer those who put it forward. This task would better suit a man versed in theology than myself, a person who knows nothing of that discipline.

Nevertheless, it is my judgment that in a matter so divine and so sublime and so far surpassing human intelligence as is this truth with which it has pleased God's goodness to enlighten us, it is crucial that he lend us his help yet further, by an extraordinary and special favor, so as to allow us to grasp it and to lodge it in us. And I do not believe that purely human means are capable of this; if they were, so many rare and excellent souls in ancient times, so abundantly furnished with natural powers, would not have failed to arrive at that knowledge in their reasoning.

It is faith alone that embraces vividly and with certainty the high mysteries of our religion. But that is not to say that it is not a very fine and very laudable enterprise, in addition, to apply the natural and human tools God has given us to the service of our faith. There can be no doubt that this is the most honorable use we could make of them and that there is no occupation or undertaking worthier of a Christian than to attempt by all his studies and reflections to embellish, extend, and amplify the truth of his belief. We are not satisfied with serving

5. Adrianus Turnebus (1512–65) was a professor at the Collège Royal.

God in mind and soul; we also owe him and render him bodily reverence; we apply our very limbs and movements and external objects to
honoring him. Similarly, we must accompany our faith with all the reason in us, but always with this reservation: we should not suppose that
faith depends on us, or that our efforts and arguments can achieve so
supernatural and divine a knowledge.

If faith does not enter into us by an extraordinary infusion, if it
enters, not to say only through reasoning, but through any human
means, it is not present in its dignity or in its splendor. And yet I am
afraid we have it only in this way. If we held to God through the mediation of a living faith, if we held to God through him, not through ourselves, if we had a divine footing and foundation, human events would
not have the power to shake us as they do; our fortunes would not be
prone to surrender to so weak an assault. The love of novelty, the subjection of princes, the success of one faction, the rash and fortuitous
change of our opinions, would not have the power to shake and alter
our belief. We would not let it be troubled by a new argument or by
persuasion—not by all the rhetoric there ever was. We should with-
stand those waves with an inflexible and immobile firmness:

> As a vast rock repels the seas that beat on it and disperses the
> roaring waves that surround it by its great bulk . . .[6]

If this ray of divinity touched us in any way, it would appear everywhere: not only our words, but our actions too, would carry its bright-
ness and its luster. We would see everything that came from us
illuminated by this noble radiance. We ought to be ashamed that in
human sects there was never a partisan, whatever difficulty and oddity
his doctrine supported, who did not in some way adapt his conduct and
his life to it; and so divine and celestial an institution [as ours] marks
Christians only by their words.

<Do you want to see this? Compare our customs to those of a
Mohammedan or a pagan; you always lag behind. This is true even
though, in view of the advantage of our religion, we ought to shine in
excellence, completely outstripping them, and people ought to say,
"Are they so just, so charitable, so good? Then they must be Christians."
<<All other appearances are common to all religions: hope, trust,
events, ceremonies, penitence, martyrs. The particular mark of our
truth should be our virtue, as it is also the most heavenly and the most
difficult, and the worthiest product of truth.>>

6. Author unknown.

Hence our good king Saint Louis was right in promptly dissuading that Tartar king who had become a Christian and who planned to go to Lyon to kiss the Pope's feet and to witness the sanctity he hoped to find in our customs. For the king feared that, on the contrary, our dissolute way of living would turn him away from so sacred a belief. And how different was the outcome for that other person, who went to Rome with the same purpose. Seeing the dissoluteness of the prelates and the people of that time, he became all the more firmly established in our religion, considering how much power and divinity it must have to maintain its dignity and its splendor among so much corruption and in such vicious hands.>

"If we had a single drop of faith," says Holy Scripture, "we would move mountains."[7] Our actions, which would be guided and accompanied by divinity, would not be simply human; they would have something miraculous about them, like our belief. <<*"It does not take long to establish an honest and blessed life, if you believe."*[8]

Some make the world believe that they believe what they do not believe. Others, in greater number, make themselves believe that they believe, without being able to penetrate into what it is to believe.>>

And we find it strange if, in the wars that now oppress our state, we see events changing and diversifying in a common, ordinary manner. The reason is that we bring to them nothing but what is our own. The justice that belongs to one of the factions is there only as ornament and coloring. It is indeed referred to, but it is neither received nor lodged nor espoused there: it is there as in the mouth of the lawyer, not as in the heart and affection of the litigant. God owes his extraordinary aid to faith and to religion, not to our passions. People are the leaders here and make use of religion. It ought to be quite the contrary.

<<See whether it is not by our hands that we guide religion, shaping contrary figures so easily from a rule so straight and so firm. Where is this better seen than in France in our day? Those who have taken it to the left, those who have taken it to the right, those who call it black, those who call it white, use it equally for their violent and ambitious enterprises, and there conduct themselves with a demeanor so uniform in debauchery and injustice, that they make it doubtful and difficult to believe the diversity they claim for their opinions in a matter on which the conduct and law of our life depends. Can one see conduct more united, more at one, issuing from the same school and discipline?

7. Matthew 17:20 and 21:21.
8. Quintilian, *Institutio oratoria*, XII, 11.

Look at the horrible impudence with which we toss about divine arguments, and how irreligiously we have both rejected them and again accepted them, according to how fortune has changed our place in these public tempests. Consider that most solemn proposition: "Whether it is permissible for the subject to rebel and take arms against his prince for the defense of religion." Remember in what mouths, this past year, its affirmation was the buttress of one party, its negation the buttress of the other. Now hear from what quarter the voice of instruction comes, and if the weapons make less noise for this side than for that. We burn people who say that truth must suffer the yoke of our necessity. But how much worse are France's actions than her words!>>

Let us confess the truth: if you took from our armies those who march there only out of zeal inspired by a religious sentiment and, in addition, those who consider only the protection of the laws of their country or the service of the prince, you could hardly make of them one whole company of soldiers. If they are not driven by particular <<and contingent>> considerations whose diversity moves them, how does it happen that so few have maintained the same will and the same demeanor in our public disturbances? That we see them now moving a step at a time, now running at full speed? And that we see the same people now spoiling our affairs by their violence and harshness, now by their coldness, softness, and sluggishness?

<<I see clearly that we willingly assign to devotion only the religious duties that flatter our passions. There is no hostility so extreme as that of the Christian. Our zeal works marvels when it seconds our inclination toward hatred, cruelty, ambition, greed, slander, and rebellion. On the other hand, it neither walks nor flies toward goodness, benevolence, temperance, if some rare complexion does not miraculously predispose it to them.

Our religion is made to eradicate vices; it covers them, nourishes them, and encourages them.>>

We must not play tricks on God. If we believed him, I do not say by faith, but by a simple belief, even (and I say this to our great confusion) if we believed him and recognized him as we would any other likely story, or as we do one of our comrades, we would love him beyond all other things for the infinite goodness and beauty that shine in him. At least he would occupy the same rank in our affection as riches, pleasures, glory, and our friends.

<<The best of us is not afraid to insult him, as he is afraid to insult his neighbor, his kinsman, his master. Is there any mind so simple that, if it had on one side the object of one of our vicious pleasures and on the other, with equal knowledge and persuasion, the state of immortal

glory, would trade one for the other? Nevertheless, we often renounce it out of pure disdain; for what preference leads us to blaspheme unless perhaps the very predilection for the offense?

When the philosopher Antisthenes was being initiated into the mysteries of Orpheus and the priest said to him that those who committed themselves to that religion were to receive eternal and perfect blessings after death, he replied, "Then why don't you die yourself?"[9]

Beyond our subject matter, Diogenes more brusquely, as was his fashion, said to the priest who was preaching at him in the same way to get him to join his order so as to acquire the blessings of the other world: "Do you want me to believe that Agesilaus and Epaminondas, such great men, will be wretched, and you, who are a mere calf, will be quite happy because you are a priest?">>[10]

As to these great promises of eternal blessedness, if we received them with the same authority we give to a philosophical discourse, we would not hold death in such horror as we do.

> <The dying man would no longer complain about his
>   dissolution,
> But would rather rejoice at going forth to shed his skin like
>   the snake
> Or as the aged stag sheds his overly long antlers.>[11]

"I want to be dissolved," we should say, "and be with Jesus Christ." The power of Plato's dialogue on the immortality of the soul did indeed push some of his disciples to their death, so that they might sooner enjoy the hopes he gave them.

All this is a very clear sign that we receive our religion in our own way and by our own hands, and no differently from the way other religions are received. We happen to find ourselves in the country where it has been practiced; or we value its antiquity or the authority of the people who have supported it; or we fear the threats it attaches to wrongdoers; or we follow its promises. These considerations should be employed to uphold our belief, but as subsidiaries: they are human bonds. By the same means another country, other witnesses, similar promises and threats, could in the same way imprint in us a contrary belief.

<We are Christians in the same way that we are Perigordians or Germans.>

9. Diogenes Laertius, *Lives*, VI, 4, "Life of Antisthenes."
10. Diogenes Laertius, *Lives*, VI, 39, "Life of Diogenes."
11. Lucretius, *De rerum natura*, III, 612–4.

And what Plato says[12] — that there are few people so firm in atheism that a pressing danger does not lead them to the recognition of divine power — this attitude in no way touches a real Christian. It is the place of mortal and human religions to be received through human guidance. What kind of faith must it be that cowardice and weakness plant and establish in us? <<A nice faith that believes what it believes only because it lacks the courage to disbelieve it!>> Can a vicious passion like inconstancy or terror produce anything regulated in our souls?

<<Through their arguments, Plato says, the atheists establish that what is told of hell and of future punishments is fictional. But when the occasion to test this occurs, as old age and illness bring them closer to death, the terror of that fills them with a new belief through dread of their future state. And because such impressions make hearts fearful, in his *Laws* he forbids all teaching of such threats and of the notion that any harm can come to man through the gods, except for his own greater good, when he lacks it, and for a medicinal effect. They tell of Bion who, infected with the atheism of Theodorus, had long been a mocker of religious men; but, when death surprised him, he gave way to the most extreme superstitions, as if the gods withdrew and returned according to the needs of Bion.[13]

Plato and these examples lead to the conclusion that we are brought back to belief in God either by love or by force. Atheism is an unnatural and monstrous proposition, difficult, too, and hard to establish in the human mind, however insolent and disordered it may be. But enough people have been seen to affect its profession outwardly, through vanity and pride in conceiving unpopular opinions meant to reform the world; these, if they are mad enough, are nevertheless not strong enough to have it fixed in their consciousness. They will not refrain from clasping their hands to heaven if you give them a good thrust with a sword in the chest. And when fear or illness has beaten down the licentious fervor of a giddy humor, they will not hesitate to return, and to conform to public beliefs and examples. A dogma seriously assimilated is one thing; those superficial impressions which, born of the debauchery of an unhinged mind, swim about rashly and uncertainly in the fancy are another. Wretched and brainless men, indeed, who attempt to be worse than they can be!>>

<The error of paganism and the ignorance of our sacred truth allowed that great soul of Plato (but great with human greatness only)

12. Plato, *Laws*, X.
13. Diogenes Laertius, *Lives*, IV, 54, "Life of Bion."

to fall also into that related error, that children and old men are more susceptible to religion, as if it arose and obtained its credit from our imbecility.>

The knot that should bind our judgment and our will, that should clasp our soul and join it to its creator, should be a knot that derives its coils and its powers, not from our considerations, from our arguments and our passions, but from a divine and supernatural constraint, there being only one form, one face, and one luster, which is the authority of God and his grace. Now, while our hearts and souls are governed and commanded by faith, it is right that it calls all our other parts to its service according to their powers. Moreover, it is not credible that this whole machine should not bear some marks imprinted by the hand of that great architect, and that there is not some image in the things of this world somehow relating to the workman who built and formed them. He has left on these lofty works the stamp of his divinity, and it is due only to our imbecility that we cannot discover it. That is what he tells us himself, that he manifests his invisible works to us through those that are visible. Sebond has worked at this worthy task and shows us how there is no part of the world that disclaims its maker.

It would offend the divine goodness if the universe did not agree with our beliefs. Heaven, earth, the elements, our body, and our soul—all things conspire in this; we have only to find the means of making use of them. They instruct us, if we are capable of understanding. <For this world is a most holy temple into which man is introduced to contemplate statues—not those made by mortal hand, but those that the divine thought has made perceptible: the sun, the stars, the waters, and the earth, to represent for us things intelligible.> "The invisible things of God," says Saint Paul, "appear through the creation of the world, when we consider his eternal wisdom and his divinity through his works."[14]

> God does not refuse the sight of the heavens to the earth.
> In making it roll ceaselessly above our heads he reveals his
>   visage and his body.
> He offers himself to us and inculcates himself in us
> In order that we may know him well.
> Finally, also, in looking on him we learn his nature and
>   learn to pay attention to his laws.[15]

14. Romans 1:20.
15. Manilius, *Astronomica*, IV, 907–11.

Now our human arguments and discussions are like heavy and barren matter; the grace of God is their form—that is what provides their style and their value. Just as the virtuous actions of Socrates and of Cato remain vain and useless, because they failed to have as their end or concern the love and obedience of the true Creator of all things, and because they did not know God, so it is with our imaginings and our discourses. They have a body of some kind, but are only an unformed mass, without shape or illumination, unless the faith and grace of God are joined to them. Faith, coming to color and light up Sebond's arguments, makes them firm and solid. They are capable of serving as an approach and first guide to an apprentice, to put him on the path to this knowledge. They shape him somehow and make him fit for the grace of God, by means of which our own belief is afterward completed and perfected. I know a man of authority, raised on letters, who confessed to me that he had been brought back from the errors of disbelief through the mediation of Sebond's arguments. And even if we strip them of that ornament and of the aid and approbation of faith and take them for purely human fantasies to combat those who have been cast into the frightful and horrible darkness of irreligion, they will still be found to be as solid and firm as any others that can be opposed to them, in such a way that we will be in a condition to say to our opponents,

If you have something better, produce it, or accept our rule,[16]

that is, suffer the force of our demonstrations or show us somewhere else, and on some other subject, some that are better woven and made of better material.

[3. Second Objection against Sebond, and Montaigne's Reply]

Without thinking, I have already become half-engaged in the second objection to which I had proposed to reply on behalf of Sebond.

Some say that his arguments are feeble and unable to confirm what he wishes, and they undertake to refute them easily. We must shake these critics a little more roughly, for they are more dangerous and more malicious than the former. <<People are apt to interpret the writings of others in favor of the opinions they themselves hold in advance; and an atheist flatters himself by relating all writings to atheism, infecting

16. Horace, *Epistles*, I, v, 6.

innocent material with his own poison.>> These people have some pre-possession in their judgment that makes them insensible to Sebond's arguments. Further, it seems to them that they are given an easy mark when they are set free to attack our religion with mere human arms, while they would not dare to attack it in its majesty, full of authority and of command.

The means that I take to beat back this frenzy, and which seems to me most appropriate, is to crush and trample underfoot human vanity and pride; to make them feel the inanity, the vanity and nothingness of man; to snatch from their hands the miserable weapons of their reason; to make them bow their heads and bite the dust beneath the authority and reverence of divine majesty. To it alone belong knowledge and wisdom; it alone can value something by its own power; from it we steal what we say about ourselves and pride ourselves on.

For God allows no one but himself to be wise.[17]

<<Let us beat down this presumption, the first foundation of the tyranny of the evil spirit. *"God resists the proud but gives grace to the humble."*>>[18] Intelligence is in all the gods, said Plato, and in very few men.[19]

However, it is a great consolation for a Christian to see our mortal and frail tools so aptly suited to our holy and divine faith that when we use them on subjects that are by their nature mortal and frail, they are not applied with any more unity or force. Let us see then if man has in his power other arguments stronger than those of Sebond and even if he has it in him to arrive at any certainty by argument and reason.

<<Saint Augustine, arguing against these people,[20] has occasion to complain of their injustice in considering false those parts of our belief that our reason fails to establish. And in order to show that many things can exist and have existed whose nature and causes our arguments cannot establish, he sets before them certain known and indubitable experiences of which man admits he understands nothing; he does this, like everything else, with painstaking and ingenious research. We must do more and teach them that there is no need to go hunting for strange examples to show convincingly the weakness of our reason: it is so deficient and so blind that there is no matter clear enough for it. The easy

17. Herodotus, VII, 10; cited by Stobaeus, *Apophthegmata*, sermo 22.
18. 1 Peter 5:5; James 4:6.
19. Plato, *Timaeus* 51e.
20. Saint Augustine, *City of God*, XXI, 5.

and the difficult are all one to our reason. All subjects equally, and nature in general, disavow its jurisdiction and its mediation.>>

What does truth preach to us when it preaches that we should flee worldly philosophy?[21] When it so often instills in us that our wisdom is but folly before God? That of all vanities, the vainest is man? That man, who boasts of his knowledge, does not even know what knowledge is?[22] And that man, who is nothing, is misleading and deceiving himself if he thinks he is something?[23] These sayings of the Holy Spirit express so clearly and so vividly what I want to maintain that I need no other proof against people who would surrender with all submission and obedience to its authority. But these people want to be whipped at their own expense and will not allow their reason to be challenged by anything other than itself.

[1. The Vanity of Man's Knowledge without God]

Let us then consider, for the moment, man alone, without external help, armed solely with his own arms, and stripped of the grace and divine knowledge that are his whole honor, his power, and the foundation of his being. Let us see what figure he cuts in this fine array. Let him make me understand, by the effort of his reasoning, on what foundations he has built these great advantages he thinks he has over other creatures.

Who has persuaded him that that marvelous motion of the celestial vault, the eternal light of those torches rolling so proudly overhead, the terrible movements of that infinite sea are established and continue for so many centuries for his convenience and for his service? Is it possible to imagine anything so ridiculous as that this wretched and cowardly creature, who is not even master of himself, exposed to threats from all things, should call himself master and emperor of the universe when he lacks the power to understand its least part, let alone to command it? And as for this privilege that he claims of being the only one in this great edifice who has the ability to recognize its beauty and its parts, the only one who can give thanks to the architect and keep accounts of the receipts and expenses of the world: who has granted him this privilege? Let him show his credentials for this fine and great charge.

<<Have they been granted in favor of the wise only? Then there are many people they do not touch. Are fools and scoundrels worthy of so

21. Colossians 2:8.
22. 1 Corinthians 8:2.
23. Galatians 6:3.

extraordinary a favor, and although they are the worst part of the world, are they worthy of being preferred to all the rest?

And shall we believe this: "*For whom then shall we say the world was made? Why, for those animate beings who have the use of reason. These are gods and men, to whom surely nothing is superior.*"[24] We can never have done enough to defy the impudence of claiming this conjunction.>>

But, poor thing, what has he in himself to merit such an advantage? Consider that incorruptible life of the celestial bodies, their beauty, their grandeur, and their continuous movements under so exact a law:

> ... *when we gaze on the celestial vaults of the vast universe*
> *Above our heads, and the ether composed of sparkling stars,*
> *When we reflect on the revolutions of the sun and moon.*[25]

Consider the dominance and power those bodies have, not only over our lives and the conditions of our lot—

> *For he makes the actions and the lives of men depend on the*
> *stars.*[26]

—but on our very inclinations, our thoughts, our acts of will, which they govern, impel, and agitate at the mercy of their influences, as our reason finds and teaches us:

> *... it recognizes*
> *That the stars we see so far away govern men by secret laws,*
> *That the whole world moves according to a periodic motion,*
> *And that the choices of our destinies are regulated by certain*
> *signs.*[27]

Observe that not only a single human being, not a king, but monarchies and empires and this whole lower world move to the rolling of the smallest celestial movements:

> *How large are the effects of the smallest motions;*
> *How great is this power that governs even kings?*[28]

24. Cicero, *De natura deorum*, II, liii; Balbus the Stoic is speaking.
25. Lucretius, *De rerum natura*, V, 1203–5.
26. Manilius, *Astronomica*, III, 58.
27. Manilius, *Astronomica*, I, 60–3.
28. Manilius, *Astronomica*, I, 55 and IV, 93.

If our virtue, our vices, our wisdom and our knowledge, and these same
speculations that we produce about the power of the stars, and this
comparison between them and us, comes, as our reason judges, by their
mediation and their favor—

> . . . one, in the transports of love,
> Crosses the sea to ruin Troy;
> Another is destined to compose laws;
> Here we have children who kill their fathers, and parents
>   their children;
> Brothers take arms for fratricidal combat.
> This war does not depend on us.
> Destiny forces men to overturn everything, to punish
>   themselves, and to lacerate their limbs.
> This, too, is fated, that I write of fate.[29]

—if we hold by the dispensation of the heavens that share of reason that
we have, how can we consider ourselves equal to them? How can we
subject their essence and their conditions to our science? All that we
see in these bodies astonishes us. <<"What were the instruments, the
levers, the machines, the ministers of so great a work?">>[30] Why do we
deny them soul and life and reason? Have we recognized in them some
immobile and insensible stupidity, we who have no commerce with
them except obedience?

<<Shall we say that we have seen in no other creature but man the
use of a rational soul? Well! Have we seen anything like the sun? Does
it stop existing because we have seen nothing like it? And do its movements cease to exist because there are none like them? If what we have
not seen does not exist, our knowledge is wonderfully reduced: "How
narrow are the limits of the mind!">>[31]

Is it not dreams of human vanity that make of the moon a celestial
earth, <<that dream up mountains and valleys (as Anaxagoras does),>>[32]
plant human habitations and dwellings, arrange colonies there for our
benefit (as Plato and Plutarch do)[33] and make of our earth a glowing
and luminous star? <<"Among other inconveniences of mortality is this:
the darkness of the understanding, not so much the need to make errors as

29. Manilius, *Astronomica*, IV, 79, 89, and 118.

30. Cicero, *De natura deorum*, I, viii.

31. Cicero, *De natura deorum*, I, xxxi.

32. Diogenes Laertius, *Lives*, II, 8, "Life of Anaxagoras."

33. Plutarch, *On the Face That Can Be Seen on the Lunar Disk*.

the love of errors."[34] *"The corruptible body weighs down the soul, and the earthly habitation oppresses the thinking mind."*>>[35]

[2. Man Is No Better than the Beasts]

Presumption is our natural and original illness. The most ill-fated and feeble of all creatures is man, and at the same time the vainest. He feels and sees himself lodged here among the mud and dung of the world, attached and nailed to the worst, deadest, and most stagnant part of the universe, on the lowest floor of the house, farthest removed from the celestial vault, in the worst condition of the three kinds of animals.[36] And there he goes, planting himself in imagination above the circle of the moon and bringing the heavens beneath his feet. It is through the vanity of that same imagination that he equates himself with God, that he attributes divine attributes to himself, picks himself out and separates himself from the crowd of other creatures, allots their shares to the animals, his brothers and companions, and distributes among them such a portion of faculties and powers as he sees fit. How does he know the internal movements and secrets of animals by the effort of his intelligence? By what comparison between them and us does he infer the stupidity that he attributes to them? <<When I play with my cat, who knows if she is making more a pastime of me than I of her?

Plato, in his account of the Golden Age under Saturn,[37] counts among the chief advantages of the man of that time the communication he had with beasts. Inquiring of them and learning from them, he knew the true qualities and differences of each of them. Thus, acquiring a very perfect intelligence and prudence, he conducted his life much more happily than we would now know how to do. Do we need better evidence to judge human impudence toward beasts? That great writer believed that nature, in giving them their bodily form, considered only the use that would be made of them in prognostications in his time.>>[38]

The same defect that prevents communication between them and us, why is it not as much our fault as theirs? We can only guess whose fault it is that we do not understand one another, for we do not understand

34. Seneca, *De ira*, II, ix.
35. Quoted by Saint Augustine, *City of God*, XII, xv.
36. I.e., aerial, aquatic, and terrestrial animals.
37. Plato, *Statesman* 272a–d.
38. Plato, *Timaeus* 72b–d.

them any more than they understand us. By the same reasoning they can consider us stupid beasts, just as we consider them. It is no great wonder that we do not understand them; no more do we understand Basques or troglodytes. Nevertheless, some people have boasted of understanding beasts, like Apollonius, Thyaneus, <Melampus, Teiresias, Thales,> and others. <And since it is the case, as naturalists tell us, that there are nations who accept a dog as their king,[39] they must have given a precise interpretation of its voice and movements.> We must take note that there is parity between us. We have some degree of understanding of their meaning and they of ours, to about the same degree. They flatter us, threaten us and implore us, and we them.

Meanwhile, we discover quite plainly that there is full and complete communication between them and that they understand one another, not only within the same species, but also across different species:

> <And the cattle lacking speech, and even the wild beasts,
> Make themselves understood with different and varied cries
> According as they feel fear, pain, or joy.>[40]

The horse recognizes anger in a certain bark of a dog. It is not frightened at another of the dog's sounds. Even in the case of beasts that have no voice, we easily recognize, through the social ties we observe among them, that they have some other means of communication. <<Their movements converse and negotiate:>>

> <It appears that, in the same way,
> Lack of speech leads infants to express themselves through
>   gestures.>[41]

Why not? Do not our mutes dispute, argue, and tell stories in the same way by means of signs? I have seen some so supple and so well-versed in this, that in fact they lacked nothing of what was needed to make themselves perfectly understood. Lovers grow angry, are reconciled, entreat, express thanks, make assignations, and indeed say everything with their eyes:

> And silence, too, records our prayers and our words.[42]

39. Pliny, Naturalis historia, VI, 35.
40. Lucretius, De rerum natura, V, 1058–60.
41. Lucretius, De rerum natura, V, 1029–30.
42. Tasso, Aminta, Act II, 34.

<<What of the hands? We plead, we promise, call, dismiss, threaten, pray, entreat, deny, refuse, question, admire, count, confess, repent, fear, show shame, doubt, instruct, command, incite, encourage, swear oaths, bear witness, accuse, condemn, absolve, insult, despise, defy, annoy, flatter, applaud, bless, humiliate, mock, reconcile, recommend, exalt, celebrate, rejoice, complain, grieve, mope, despair, express astonishment, exclaim, keep silent—and what do we not do?—with a variety and multiplicity that rivals language. With the head, we invite, dismiss, avow, disavow, deny, welcome, honor, revere, disdain, question, reject, cheer, lament, caress, scold, submit, defy, exhort, menace, assure, inquire. What of the eyebrows? What of the shoulders? There is no movement that does not speak a language intelligible without instruction and at the same time a common language. In view of the variety and distinctive idiom of other languages, this means that sign language must be judged the language proper to human nature. I leave aside what necessity teaches promptly to those in need, and the alphabets of the fingers and the grammar of gestures, and the branches of learning that are exercised and expressed only through gesture, as well as the nations that Pliny says have no other tongue.>>[43]

<An ambassador of the city of Abdera, after speaking at length to King Agis of Sparta, asked him: "Well, Sire, what reply do you wish me to take back to our citizens?"—"That I let you say all that you wanted, and as much as you wanted, without saying a word."[44] Is that not an eloquent and truly intelligible silence?>

Further, what sort of capacity of ours do we not recognize in the actions of animals? Is there a polity better ordered, with more varied positions and offices, and more constantly maintained than that of the honeybees? Can we imagine that this so well-ordered disposition of actions and functions can be conducted without reason and foresight?

> *To these signs and before these examples, some have said*
> *That the bees partake of the divine mind and ethereal*
> *breath.*[45]

Do the swallows we see returning in the spring and exploring every corner of our houses search without judgment and choose without discernment from a thousand places the one most convenient for their nest? And in their lovely and admirably woven constructions, can birds

43. Pliny, *Naturalis historia*, VI, 30.
44. Plutarch, *Sayings of the Lacedaemonians* (trans. Amyot).
45. Virgil, *Georgics*, IV, 219–21.

make use of a square rather than a round shape, of an obtuse rather than a right angle, without knowing their properties and their effects? Do they take now water, now clay, without judging that hardness is softened by moisture? Do they carpet their palace with moss or with down, without foreseeing that the tender limbs of their little ones will lie there more softly and more comfortably? Do they protect themselves from the rainy wind and make their habitation face the east, without knowing the different characters of these winds and considering that the one is better for them than the other? Why does the spider thicken its web in one place and loosen it in another, use one kind of knot this time and another at another time, if it does not have deliberation and thought and powers of inference? We see readily enough in most of their works how much superiority the animals have over us and how feeble is our art when it comes to imitating them. Nevertheless, we discern in our cruder works the faculties that we employ in them and that our soul applies itself in all its powers. Why do we not judge the same of them? Why do we attribute to some sort of natural and servile inclination the works that surpass everything we can do by nature and by art? In this, without realizing it, we give them a very great advantage over us in making nature, with maternal tenderness, accompany and guide them as if by the hand in all the actions and comforts of their life. And as for us, nature abandons us to chance and fortune, and makes us seek through art the things necessary for our preservation. And at the same time nature refuses us the means of being able to arrive, by any instruction or effort of the understanding, at the natural industry of beasts, so that their brutal stupidity surpasses, in all circumstances, everything that our divine invention and our arts can do.

Indeed, in this respect, we would have good reason to call her a cruel stepmother. But that is not so. The way we are organized is not so deformed and so monstrous. Nature has embraced all her creatures without exception. There is none that she has not fully furnished with all the means necessary to the conservation of its existence. What of the common complaints I have heard made about men (as the license of their opinions now raises them above the clouds and then plunges them to the antipodes)? They say we are the only animal abandoned naked on the naked earth, tied, bound, given nothing to arm or cover ourselves with except what we can plunder from others. On the other hand, nature has adorned all other creatures with shells, husks, bark, hair, wool, spikes, hide, down, feathers, scales, fleece, or silk, according to the needs of their being. She has armed them with talons, teeth, or horns with which to attack and defend themselves. She has herself instructed them in what is proper to them, swimming, running, flying,

and singing. Whereas without instruction, man does not know how to
walk or speak or eat or do anything but cry:

> <When the infant, like the mariner cast on the shore by the
>   cruel waves,
> Lies on the earth, naked, without speech, deprived of
>   everything
> That would help him live, from the moment when nature has
>   snatched him
> With effort from the womb of his mother onto the shores of
>   light,
> He fills the place of his birth with wailing,
> As is right for one to whom it remains to bear so many ills in
>   life.
> In contrast, farm animals, large and small, and wild beasts
>   grow painlessly.
> They have no need of rattles or of the little words of affection
>   of a tender nurse.
> They do not change their clothing with the season.
> Finally, they have no need of armament or of high walls
> To protect their goods since earth itself and nature,
> Ingenious contriver, provide all things to all of them.>[46]

These laments are false. There is greater equality and more uniform
relationship in the constitution of the world.

Our skin is provided as well as theirs with solidity against the insults
of the weather: witness the many nations that have never yet sampled
the use of clothing. <Our ancient Gauls were scantily clad; so are our
neighbors, the Irish, under so cold a sky.> But we can judge better from
ourselves, for all the places on our person we choose to expose to the
wind and the air are found fit to endure it: face, feet, hands, legs, shoulders, head, as custom dictates. For if there is a part of us that is weak
and seems to fear the cold, it would have to be the stomach, where
digestion takes place. Our fathers left it uncovered, and our ladies, delicate as they are, sometimes go barely covered as far as the navel. Binding and swaddling of infants are not necessary either: witness the
Spartan mothers who raised their children with complete freedom of
movement for their limbs without tying or wrapping them.[47] Our crying

---

46. Lucretius, *De rerum natura*, V, 223–35.
47. Plutarch, *Lives*, XIII, "Life of Lycurgus."

is shared by most of the other animals, and there is hardly one of them
that we do not see complaining and groaning long after they are born,
since it is behavior wholly appropriate to the weakness they feel. As to
the habit of eating, it is in us, as in them, natural and does not have to
be learned:

> <For each one takes account of his own powers.>[48]

Who doubts that an infant who has grown strong enough to feed himself would know how to look for food? And the earth produces and
offers him food sufficient for his need, without cultivation or artifice—
perhaps not in every season, but neither does it do that for the beasts:
witness the provisions that we see ants and other creatures making for
the sterile times of the year. Those nations we have just discovered so
abundantly furnished with natural food and drink, without cultivation
or preparation, have just taught us that bread is not our only nourishment. Our Mother Nature has furnished us in abundance with all that
we need—indeed, as seems likely, even more fully and more richly
than she does now that we have mixed our skills with it:

> At first the earth itself spontaneously brought forth
> Lustrous harvests and smiling vineyards;
> Of herself she gave the sweet fruits and smiling pastures
> That now grow with great pain at the price of our labor,
> Exhausting our oxen and the strength of our farmers.[49]

The excess and unruliness of our appetite outstrip all the inventions
that we seek to satisfy it.

As for weapons, we have more of them by nature than most other
animals, more different movements of our limbs, and we make more
use of them, naturally and without instruction. We see those who are
trained to fight in the nude confront the same dangers we do. If some
animals surpass us in this advantage, we surpass in this respect a number of others. And we have by natural instinct and precept the ingenuity
to strengthen and protect the body by external means. Note how the
elephant sharpens and whets the teeth he uses in combat (for he has
some particularly for that purpose, which he spares and uses for no
other service). When bulls go into combat, they spread and toss the

---

48. Lucretius, *De rerum natura*, V, 1032.
49. Lucretius, *De rerum natura*, II, 1157–61.

dust around them. Boars sharpen their tusks, and the ichneumon, when it is to come to grips with the crocodile, arms its body, covers it all over with a crust of mud, well-caked and kneaded, as if it were a cuirass. Why shall we not say that it is just as natural for us to arm ourselves with wood and iron?

As for speech, it is certain that, if it is not natural, it is not necessary. Nevertheless, I believe that a child who grew up entirely alone, far from all communication (this would be a difficult experiment to carry out), would have some sort of speech to express its thoughts. It is not credible that nature would have refused us the means that she has given so many other animals. For what is speech other than that capacity we see in them of complaining, rejoicing, summoning one another for help, inviting each other to love, as they do by the use of their voice? <How could they fail to speak among themselves? They speak to us and we to them. In how many ways do we speak to our dogs? And they answer us. We converse with them in a different language, with other words, from those we use with birds, with swine, with cattle, with horses. And we change our idiom according to the species:>

> *Thus in their dark swarm, one ant greets another,*
> *Perhaps to tell of their path or of their booty.*[50]

It seems to me that Lactantius attributes not only speech but also laughter to beasts. Further, the differences in language from country to country are also found in animals of the same species. Aristotle refers in this connection to the way the call of partridges varies according to their location.

> <. . . *various birds*
> *Emit very different notes at different times,*
> *And some make their songs more raucous*
> *According to the seasons.*>[51]

However, it is yet to be known what language that child would speak; and conjectures about it are not very plausible. If someone claims against this opinion that those who are deaf from birth do not speak at all, I reply that that is not only because they have not been able to be taught speech by ear. Rather it is because the sense of hearing, of which they are deprived, is related to that of speech. The two are held

---

50. Dante, *Divine Comedy, Purgatory*, XXVI, 34.
51. Lucretius, *De rerum natura*, V, 1077–80.

together by a natural bond, so that, whatever we say, we must first say it to ourselves and make it heard by our ears before sending it to the ears of others.

I have said all this to emphasize the resemblance there is to matters human and to bring us back into conformity with the majority. We are neither above nor below the rest. Everything under the sun, says the sage,[52] follows the same law and the same destiny:

> *<All things are bound by their fateful chains.>*[53]

There is some difference. There are orders and degrees, but it is all under the aspect of a single nature:

> *<Everything develops according to its own character, and all*
> *Keep the differences that the fixed laws of nature have*
> *   established between them.>*[54]

Man must be constrained and held within the limits of this order. The wretch is really not in a condition to overstep them. He is hobbled and bound. He is subject to the same obligation as other creatures of his order, and of a very mediocre condition, without any real, essential prerogative or preeminence. What he gives himself in his own opinion and fancy has neither body nor taste. And if it is the case that he alone of all the animals has this freedom of imagination and this unruliness in his thoughts, representing to himself what is, what is not, and what he wishes—the false and the true—this is an advantage that has been dearly bought, giving him little to boast about. For from it flows the principal source of the evils that beset him: sin, illness, irresolution, affliction, and despair.

To return to my subject: I say, therefore, that there is no evident reason to consider that beasts perform through natural instinct and obligation the same operations that we perform through our choice and industry. From like effects we must infer like faculties, and confess in consequence that the same intelligence, the same way we have of working, is also that of the animals. Why do we imagine that natural constraint in them, we who feel no similar effect? Consider, too, that it is more honorable, and closer to divinity, to be guided and required to act in an ordered way by a natural and inevitable condition, rather than to

52. Ecclesiastes 9:2.
53. Lucretius, *De rerum natura*, V, 574.
54. Lucretius, *De rerum natura*, V, 921–2.

act in that way through a presumptuous and fortuitous freedom. It is safer to leave to nature rather than to us the reins of our conduct. The vanity of our presumption makes us prefer owing our competence to our own powers rather than to nature's liberality. And we enrich the other animals with natural goods and renounce them in their favor, in order to honor and ennoble ourselves with goods that have been acquired. We do this simple-mindedly, it seems to me, for I would value just as highly graces that were all mine and inborn, as those I have had to beg for and acquire by apprenticeship. It is not in our power to acquire a finer testimonial than to be favored by God and nature.

Take the fox, for example, which the inhabitants of Thrace use when they want to try to cross a frozen river on the ice. They turn it loose ahead of them for this purpose. Were we to see it at the water's edge, putting its ear very close to the ice, in order to find out whether it can hear the water running underneath far away or nearby, discovering whether there is more or less thickness in the ice, whether to retreat or advance, would we not have reason to judge that the same reasoning that takes place in our case passes through its head, and that it is a process of reasoning and deduction drawn by its natural sense: "What makes a noise is moving; what moves is not frozen; what is not frozen is liquid; and what is liquid gives way under a weight?" For to attribute that solely to a keenness of the sense of hearing, without reasoning and without inference, is a chimera and cannot enter into our imagination. We must make the same judgment about all the kinds of tricks and inventions by which animals protect themselves against the attacks we make on them.

And if we want to derive some advantage from the fact that it is in us to seize them, to make use of them, and to do what we like with them, this is only the same advantage that we have over one another. We have our slaves in this way. <Were not the Climacides those women in Syria who served, crouching on all fours, as footstools and stepladders for ladies to climb into their coaches?> Most free people surrender their lives and their being to the power of others for very slight advantages. <<The wives and concubines of the Thracians compete as to who should be chosen to be killed at her husband's tomb.>>

Have tyrants ever failed to find enough men pledged to devote themselves to them, some adding as well the necessity to accompany them into death as in life? <Whole armies have been under this obligation to their captains. The form of oath in the rough school of gladiators bore these promises: "We swear to let ourselves be bound, burned, beaten, and killed with the sword and to suffer all that legitimate gladiators suffer from their master, most religiously pledging body and soul in his service":

> *Burn my head if you like, pierce my body with steel,*
> *And scourge my back with twisted cord!*[55]

This was an obligation, indeed; and yet in a given year there were ten thousand who entered into it and were lost.>

<<When the Scythians buried their king, they strangled on his body the most favored of his concubines, his cupbearer, the master of his stable, his chamberlain, the usher of his chamber, and his cook. And on the anniversary [of his death] they killed fifty horses mounted by fifty pages whom they had impaled from spine to throat, and left them thus planted on display around the tomb.>>

Those who serve us do so more cheaply and for a less careful and favorable treatment than we give to birds, horses, and dogs. <<To what lowly tasks do we not stoop for their comfort? The most abject servants do not seem to me to do willingly for their masters what princes take pride in doing for these beasts.

When Diogenes saw his parents taking pains to free him from servitude, he said, "They are mad, for he who keeps and feeds me is he who serves me."[56] And those who keep animals should be said to serve them rather than to be served by them.>> And yet animals are more high-minded, since no lion ever enslaved itself to another lion, nor a horse to another horse, for lack of courage.

As we hunt animals, so tigers and lions hunt men. And they practice the same exercise on one another: dogs chase after hares, pike after tench, swallows after grasshoppers, sparrow hawks after blackbirds and larks:

> <*. . . the stork feeds her little ones*
> *On snakes and lizards that she finds in hidden places,*
> *And in the woodlands those noble birds, the eagles, servants*
>   *of Jove,*
> *Hunt the hare and the roe.*[57]

We share the fruit of the hunt with our dogs and birds, as we do the trouble and effort. And beyond Amphipolis in Thrace, hunters and wild falcons divide the booty exactly in half. Similarly, along Lake Maotis, if the fisherman does not honestly leave an equal share of his catch to the wolves, they straightway tear up his nets.>

55. Tibullus, *Poems*, I, ix, 21–2.
56. Diogenes Laertius, *Lives*, VI, 75, "Life of Diogenes."
57. Juvenal, *Satires*, XIV, 71–4.

Further, as we have a kind of hunt that is carried out more by subtlety than by force, as with snares and lines and hooks, so similar
devices are also seen among animals. Aristotle says that the cuttlefish
throws out from its neck a long gut for a line, extending it to full length
when releasing it, and pulling it back into itself when it wants to. When
the cuttlefish hiding in the sand or the mud becomes aware of a little
fish approaching, it lets the fish nibble the end of the gut, and little by
little it withdraws the gut until the little fish is so close that it can catch
it with one spring.

As to strength, there is no animal in the world exposed to so many
injuries as man. We do not need a whale, an elephant or a crocodile, or
other animals of that kind, any one of which can destroy a great number
of men. Lice are enough to send the dictatorship of Sylla into recess.
The heart and life of a great and triumphant emperor are but the break-
fast of a little worm.

Why do we say that science and knowledge built by art and reasoning allow man to distinguish the things useful to him and of assistance
in his illnesses, from those that are not? And that it is through these that
we know the power of rhubarb and of fern? We see the goats of Candia,
when wounded by an arrow, choose dittany for their cure out of a mil-
lion herbs. We see the tortoise, when it has eaten a viper, at once look
for oregano to purge itself. The dragon rubs and clears its eyes with fen-
nel. Storks give themselves enemas of seawater. Elephants extract jave-
lins and darts that have been hurled at them in combat, not only from
their own bodies and those of their comrades, but from the bodies of
their masters (witness the case of King Porus, whom Alexander
defeated), and extract them so dexterously that we could not do it with
so little pain. Why do we not say, in the same way, that this is science
and practical wisdom? For to claim, to their detriment, that it is only
through the instruction and mastery of nature that they know this, is not
to deprive them of the title of knowledge and practical wisdom. It is to
attribute it to them more correctly than to us, in honor of so infallible a
schoolmistress.

Chrysippus, in other matters, was as contemptuous a judge of the
condition of animals as any other philosopher. However, in the case of
the dog that finds itself at a crossing of three roads when in pursuit of the
master it has lost, or when chasing some prey running away from it—the
dog goes and tries one road after the other, and when it has made sure of
two of them and found no trace of what it is looking for, it rushes into
the third without haggling—even Chrysippus is forced to admit that
some such reasoning as this takes place in that dog: "I have followed my
master's track to this crossroad. He is bound to take one of these three

roads. He hasn't gone by this one or that one. So he has to be taking that other one." And, assuring itself by this conclusion and this reasoning, the dog no longer has to rely on its sense of smell on the third road or to test it further, but allows itself to be swept on by the force of its reason. This purely dialectical action and this use of divided and conjoined propositions and of adequate enumeration of parts: is it not as valuable for the dog to have learned it from nature as from Trapezuntius?[58]

Moreover, animals are not incapable of being taught in our way. We teach blackbirds, crows, magpies, and parrots to speak. And the ease with which we see them make their voice and their breath so supple and manageable for us, so as to form and constrain it to a certain number of letters and syllables, shows that they have within them a [kind of] reasoning that makes them so docile and willing to learn. Everyone is tired, I believe, of seeing how many kinds of tricks trainers teach their dogs: the dances where they never miss a single cadence of the sound they hear, the various different movements and leaps that they are made to perform at their masters' word. But I notice with more astonishment the action of the dogs used by the blind in country and city, something nevertheless common enough. I have noticed how they stop at certain doors where they are accustomed to receiving alms, how they avoid the impact of coaches and carts, even when for their part they have enough room to pass. I have seen one of them, along a city ditch, leaving a flat, even path and taking a more inconvenient one in order to keep his master away from the ditch. How could anyone have made that dog understand that it was its task to consider only the safety of its master and to neglect its own comfort in order to serve him? And how did it know that a certain road would be quite broad enough for it, but would not be so for a blind man? Can all this be understood without ratiocination and without thought?

We must not forget what Plutarch says he saw a dog doing at Rome with the emperor Vespasian (the elder) in the theater of Marcellus. This dog served a comic who was performing a play with several scenes and several parts, and it had a role. Among other things it had to play dead for some time, after eating a certain drug. After swallowing the bread that allegedly contained the drug, it soon began to tremble and shake as if dazed. Finally, stretching out and stiffening as if dead, it let itself be pulled and dragged from one place to another, as the subject of the play demanded. And then, when the dog knew it was time, it began first to stir very gently, as if it had awakened from a profound sleep and,

58. Referring to Georgius Trapezuntius (1395–1483), author of logic texts.

lifting its head, looked here and there in a manner that astonished all those present.

The oxen that served in the royal gardens of Susa by watering them and turning certain large water wheels to which buckets were attached (like those that are often seen in Languedoc), had been ordered to do a hundred turns of the wheel a day. They were so used to that number that it was impossible to force them to turn one more time. When they had done their job, they stopped dead. We are in adolescence before we know how to count to a hundred, and we have recently discovered nations with no knowledge of numbers.

We need even more reasoning to teach another than to be taught. Now, Democritus concluded and demonstrated that the beasts have taught us most of the arts: like the spider, weaving and sewing; the swallow, building; the swan and the nightingale, music; and a number of animals, through our imitation of them, the practice of medicine. Setting that aside, Aristotle holds that nightingales teach their little ones to sing, and take time and care at it, from which it comes about that those we raise in cages, who have no chance to go to school under their parents, lose much of the grace of their song. <From this we can judge that the song improves with teaching and study. And even among free birds it is not one and the same; each has acquired it according to its capacity, and, in the jealousy of their apprenticeship, they contend in emulation of one another in a struggle so courageous that sometimes the loser dies, breath failing it before its voice. The young ruminate in pensive mood and take to imitating certain couplets of song. The pupil listens to the lesson of its teacher and gives an account of it with great care. They are silent, now one, now the other. We hear faults corrected, and perceive occasional rebukes from the teacher. I once saw, says Arrius, an elephant who had a cymbal hanging from each thigh and another attached to its trunk. The other elephants danced in a circle to this sound, rising and bowing in certain cadences, as the instrument guided them, and it was a pleasure to hear this harmony.> In the spectacles of Rome, elephants were usually seen trained to move and dance to the sound of the voice—dances with intricate movements, interruptions, and cadences very difficult to learn. Some have been seen going over their lesson in private and practicing with care and diligence in order not to be scolded and beaten by their masters.

But this other story of the magpie, for which we have Plutarch himself as witness, is strange. It lived in a barber's shop at Rome and did wonders in imitating with its voice all that it heard. One day some trumpeters happened to stop and blow for a long time in front of the shop. After that, and all the next day, there was that magpie pensive, silent and melancholy, at which everyone marveled; the sound of the trumpets was thought to have deafened and astonished it and to have totally extinguished its voice along with its hearing. But it was found in the end that the magpie was in a profound study and retreat into itself, while its mind was practicing and preparing its voice to represent the sound of the trumpets, so that its first sound was one that expressed perfectly their refrains, their pitches, and their nuances, in view of what it had newly learned, abandoning and despising all it had previously known how to say.

I do not want to omit mentioning also that other example of a dog, which this same Plutarch had seen when he was on a ship (for as to order, I know very well that I infringe on it, but I observe it no more in arranging these examples than in the rest of my work). This dog, having trouble reaching the oil that was in the bottom of a jug, where he could not get at it with his tongue because of the narrow mouth of the vessel, went to look for some pebbles and put some of them into the jug until it made the oil rise closer to the rim, where he could reach it. Now what is that but the product of a very subtle mind? It is said that the crows of Barbary do the same thing when the water they want to drink is too low.

This action is rather like that told of elephants by a king of their country, Juba, to the effect that when, thanks to the cleverness of those hunting them, one of them found itself caught in certain deep ditches that are prepared for them and covered with small branches to fool them, its companions diligently brought it large stones and pieces of wood to help it get out. But this animal recalls human capacity in so many other actions that, if I wanted to itemize what experience has taught us about it, I would easily win the argument that I usually uphold: that there is more difference between one particular man and another than there is between a particular animal and a particular man. In a private house in Syria, the keeper of an elephant robbed it at all its meals of half the amount allotted to it. One day the master decided to look after things himself, and put into the manger the right amount of barley that he had prescribed for its provender. The elephant, casting an evil eye on its keeper, separated half with its trunk, thus announcing the wrong that had been done to it. And another elephant, who had a keeper who mixed stones in its feed to increase the quantity, approached the pot in which he was cooking the meat for his dinner and filled it with ashes. Those are particular cases; but what everyone has seen, and what everyone knows, is that in all the armies that came from the Levant, one of the largest forces was composed of elephants—from whom results were obtained greater than we produce now with

our artillery—who more or less take their place in an ordered battle
(this is easy to ascertain for those who know the ancient histories):

> *<... their ancestors used to serve*
> *Hannibal of Carthage, and our leaders, and the Molossian*
> *king,*
> *And carry cohorts on their backs and the troops going into*
> *battle,*
> *Taking part in the war.>*[59]

People must have been aware of relying on their confidence in those
beasts and their reasoning, abandoning to them the front place in a battle, where the slightest stop they might have thought of making,
because of the size and weight of their bodies, the slightest fright that
might have made them turn their backs on their people, would have
been enough to lose all; and fewer cases have been observed where this
happened, that they turned back on their own troops, than where we
ourselves turn back on one another and give ground. They were given
charge, not of one simple movement, but of several different parts of
the engagement. <That was similar to what, in the recent conquest of
the Indies, the Spanish did with their dogs, to whom they paid wages
and with whom they shared their booty; and these animals showed as
much ingenuity and judgment in pursuing their victory and in holding
back from it, in charging or in retreating as the occasion demanded, in
distinguishing friends from enemies, as they did ardor and ferocity.>
We admire and give more weight to strange things than to familiar
ones. Otherwise I would not have amused myself with this long list, for,
in my opinion, anyone who looks closely at what we ordinarily see in
the animals living among us will have enough to find events just as
remarkable as what people find who go round collecting in alien countries and centuries. <<It is one and the same nature that runs its course.
If anyone had judged well enough of the present state, he could certainly infer from this both the whole of the future and the whole of the
past.>>[60] I have formerly seen among us men who had come by sea
from distant countries; who of us would not have thought them savages
and brutes, since we did not in the least understand their language and
since, as well, their manner and their countenance and their clothes

---

59. Juvenal, *Satires*, XII, 107–10.

60. Earlier editions have instead: "We live, both they and we, under the same
cover and breathe the same air; except for differences of degree, there is a constant resemblance between us."

were so distant from ours? Who would not attribute it to stupidity and silliness on seeing them speechless, ignorant of the French language, ignorant of our hand-kissing and our deep bows, our carriage and our bearing, which human nature, without fail, must take as its model?

We condemn everything that seems strange to us and that we do not understand, as it happens in the judgment we make of animals. They have several characteristics related to ours. From these, by making comparisons, we can elicit some conjectures; but as to what they have peculiar to themselves, do we know what it is? Horses, dogs, cattle, sheep, birds, and most of the animals that live with us recognize our voice and let themselves be guided by it. Crassus' moray did that and came when he called it, and so do the eels found in the fountain of Arethusa. <And I have seen enough ponds where the fish rush up to eat at a certain call from those who look after them:>

> . . . they have a name, and each of them when summoned
> Comes at his own master's voice.[61]

We can judge of that. We can also say that elephants participate to a certain extent in religion, insofar as, after certain rituals of bathing and purification, we see them stand for a long time in meditation and contemplation at certain hours of the day, without instruction or precept, lifting their trunks like arms and holding their eyes fixed toward the rising sun. But for want of seeing such an appearance in other animals, we cannot nevertheless establish that they are without religion or grasp to any extent what is hidden from us. Just as we see something in this action, which the philosopher Cleanthes noticed, because it resembles our own: He saw, he says, "ants leaving their anthill carrying the body of a dead ant to another anthill from which several other ants came forward as if to speak for them, and after they had been together for some time, the latter returned to consult, so one would suppose, with their fellow citizens, and made two or three such trips due to the difficulty of capitulating; finally, those who had come last brought the first a worm from their lair, as if for a ransom for the corpse, which worm the first ants loaded on their backs and took home, leaving to the others the body of the deceased." That is the interpretation Cleanthes gave, thus testifying that those who have no voice do not fail to have mutual interaction and communication in which it is our fault that we are not participants; and so we are meddling foolishly when we give an opinion about it.

61. Martial, *Epigrams*, IV, xxix, 6.

Now they perform still other actions that far surpass our capacity, and which we are so far from being able to imitate that we cannot conceive of them even in imagination. A number of people maintain that in that great final naval battle, which Antony lost to Augustus, his main galley was stopped in the middle of its course by that little fish the Latins call *remora* because of its habit of stopping every vessel to which it attaches itself. And when the Emperor Caligula was sailing with a great fleet on the coast of Romania, his galley alone was brought up short by this same fish, which he caused to have caught, attached as it was to the bottom of his vessel, very indignant that so small an animal could overpower the sea and the winds and the force of all his oars just by being attached by its beak to the galley (for it is a shellfish); and he was further astonished, not without reason, by the fact that when it was brought to him inside the boat, it no longer had the power that it had outside.

A citizen of Cyzicus once acquired the reputation of being a good mathematician because he had learned from the behavior of the hedgehog that it leaves its burrow open at different places and to different winds, and when it anticipates the wind's coming, it proceeds to close its hole on the side of that wind. Noticing this, that citizen provided his city with certain predictions of the wind that was going to blow. The chameleon takes the color of the place where it is sitting, but the octopus assumes for itself whatever color it likes, according to the occasion, to hide from what it fears or to catch what it is hunting. In the chameleon it is a passive change, but in the octopus it is an active one. We have some alterations of color from fright, anger, shame, and other passions that change our complexion, but that is something we suffer, as with the chameleon. It is indeed in the power of jaundice to turn us yellow, but it is not at the disposal of our will. Now these effects that we recognize in other animals, greater than our own, testify to some more excellent faculty in them hidden from us, as it is probable that there are other characteristics and powers of theirs <<of which no trace comes through to us.>>

Of all the predictions in times past, the most ancient and the most certain were those that were drawn from the flight of birds. We have nothing similar or so admirable. That rule, that order in the flapping of their wings from which consequences are drawn about things to come, must be conducted by some excellent means to yield so noble an operation, for it is playing with words to attribute so great an effect to some natural disposition without the intelligence, consent, and reasoning of the one producing it; and this is a plainly false opinion. Notice: the torpedo fish not only has the ability to numb the limbs that directly touch it, but through nets and seines it transmits a numb heaviness to the hands of those who agitate and manipulate it. Indeed, they also say that if you pour water on it, you feel through the water that sensation which comes up as far as the hand and numbs the sense of touch. This force is marvelous, but it is not useless to the torpedo. The fish is aware of it and uses it in such a way that, to catch the prey it is after, you see it hide itself under the mud, so that the other fishes swimming by above, struck and numbed by its chill, fall into its power. Cranes, swallows, and other birds of passage, changing their domicile according to the seasons of the year, show well enough the knowledge they have of their power of divination, and put it to use. Hunters assure us that to choose from a number of pups the one it is best to keep, one need only put the mother in a position to make the choice herself, since, if you take them from their kennel, the first she brings back will always be the best. Or if you pretend to surround it with fire, the first of the litter she runs to rescue will always be the best. From this it appears that they have a power of prognostication we do not have, or that they have some ability, different and livelier than ours, to judge their young.

Since the beasts' manner of being born, begetting, being nourished, acting, moving, living, and dying is so close to ours, everything we subtract from the causes that move them, and everything we add to our abilities to raise those abilities above theirs, cannot in any way arise from the workings of our reason. To regulate our health, physicians propose to us the example of the life of beasts and their behavior, for this word has always been in the mouth of the people:

> Keep feet and head warm,
> Meanwhile, live like a beast!

Generation is the principal natural action: we have a certain disposition of members that is most appropriate for this; however, they instruct us to assume a bestial posture and disposition as more effective:

>   *. . . for the most part,*
> *Women are thought to conceive best in the manner of beasts*
>   *and in the fashion of quadrupeds,*
> *For it is thus that the semen attains its goal,*
> *Chest low, loins raised up.*[62]

And they reject as harmful those indiscreet and insolent movements that women have introduced on their own, reminding them of the

62. Lucretius, *De rerum natura*, IV, 1261–4.

more modest and more composed example and practice of animals of their sex:

> *For a woman prevents herself from conceiving,*
> *If, rejoicing, with her rump she withdraws her mound of*
>   *Venus from the man,*
> *And stirs up the flow while wriggling her flanks.*
> *Thus he moves the plowshare from its proper furrow,*
> *And turns aside the thrust of the semen from its goal.*[63]

If it is justice to render each his due, the beasts, who love, serve, and defend their benefactors, and who pursue and attack strangers and those who injure them, display in this a certain aura of our justice, as they do also in maintaining a most equitable equality in the dispensation of their goods to their little ones. As to friendship, they have it, beyond comparison, in a livelier and more constant fashion than do men. When its master died, King Lysimachus' dog Hircanus remained obstinately under his bed without wanting to drink or eat; and, the day they burned his body, it ran along and threw itself into the fire, where it was burned. And so did the dog of someone called Pyrrhus, for it did not budge from its master's bed after he was dead; and when they took the body away, it let itself be carried off, too, and finally threw itself on the pyre where they were burning its master's body. There are certain inclinations of affection that sometimes arise in us without the advice of reason, which come from a fortuitous rashness others call sympathy; the beasts are capable of it, like us. We see horses acquire a certain intimacy with one another to the point of making it difficult to have them live or travel separately; we see them apply their affection to a certain coat color in their companions, as it were to a certain face, and when they encounter that color, they at once approach it with joy and demonstrations of good will and receive some other coat color with dislike and hatred. Animals, like us, have a choice in their loves and make some selection among their females. They are not exempt from our jealousies and from cases of extreme and irreconcilable envy.

Desires are natural and necessary, like drinking and eating, or natural and not necessary, like intimacy with women, or they are neither natural nor necessary. Of this last sort are almost all those of men; they are all superfluous and artificial. For it is wonderful how little nature needs in order to be satisfied, how little she has left for us to desire. The preparations of our cuisine have nothing to do with her governance.

---

63. Lucretius, *De rerum natura*, IV, 1266–9.

The Stoics say that a man could keep going on one olive a day. The delicacy of our wines is not of her teaching, nor is the surplus we add to our amorous appetites

> . . . nor does she
> Demand private parts born of a consul.[64]

These alien desires, which ignorance of the good and a false opinion have poured into us, are of so great a number that they drive out almost all the natural ones, neither more nor less than if, in a city, there were so many strangers that they drove out all the native inhabitants or extinguished their authority and ancient power, usurping it entirely and seizing it for themselves. Animals are much more restrained than we are and contain themselves with more moderation within the limits that nature has prescribed to us all, but not so exactly that they do not have something similar to our debauches. And just as there occur furious desires that impel men to the love of beasts, so they too sometimes find themselves taken with the love of us and embrace monstrous affections across species. Witness the elephant who was the rival of Aristophanes the grammarian for the love of a young flower girl in the city of Alexandria. The elephant did not yield in anything to him in the offices of a truly passionate suitor. For, strolling along the market where fruit was sold, it took some with its trunk and brought the fruit to her; it lost sight of her as little as possible and would put its trunk onto her bosom beneath her collar and feel her breasts. They also tell of a dragon that was in love with a girl, and a goose smitten with love for a child in the city of Asopus, and a ram who courted the minstrel girl Glaucia; and every day we see monkeys furiously enamored of women. We also see certain animals given to love of males of their own sex. Oppianus and others recount several examples to show the reverence that beasts feel to kin in their marriages, but experience often shows us the contrary:

> . . . the heifer submits
> To her father without shame; his daughter mates with the
>   stallion;
> The goat covers those it has produced,
> And the bird herself conceives by the very one from which
>   she has sprung.[65]

64. Horace, Satires, I, ii, 69–70.
65. Ovid, Metamorphoses, X, 325–8.

Of malicious subtlety, is there a case plainer than that of the philosopher Thales' mule? The mule, happening to stumble when crossing a
river while loaded with salt, so that the sacks it was carrying were
soaked, and noticing that the salt melted by this means had lightened
its burden, never failed, when it came to any stream, to dive into it with
its load. Eventually its master, discovering its malice, ordered that it be
loaded with wool. So the mule, finding it had miscalculated, stopped
using that maneuver. There are a number of animals who naively display the appearance of our avarice, for we see in them an extreme care
to take hold of all they can and hide it ingeniously, even though they
have no use for it.

As for household management, animals not only surpass us in their
foresightedness in amassing and saving for the time to come, but they
also have many parts of the knowledge necessary for it. Ants spread their
grains and seeds outside their threshing floor in order to air, freshen,
and dry them when they perceive that they are beginning to go moldy
and smell rancid, for fear of their spoiling and rotting. But the caution
and care they use in gnawing the grain of wheat surpasses anything
human prudence can imagine. Because the grain does not always
remain dry or wholesome, but grows soft and soggy and dissolves as in
milk, beginning to germinate and grow, they gnaw the end from which
the germ usually emerges, for fear it may sprout and lose its nature and
fitness as a storehouse for their nourishment.

As for war, which is the greatest and most solemn of human actions,
I would like to know if we want to use it as an argument for some prerogative, or, on the contrary, as evidence of our imbecility and imperfection; as indeed our knowledge of how to defeat and slaughter one
another, to ruin and destroy our own species, seems to have little attrac-
tion for the beasts who do not have it:

> <. . . when did a stronger
> Lion kill a lion? And in what wood did a boar
> Ever perish by the teeth of a stronger boar?>[66]

But they are not universally exempt from this—witness the furious
encounters of honeybees and the undertakings of the princes of two
opposing armies:

> . . . sometimes
> A great combat arises between two rulers;

66. Juvenal, *Satires*, XV, 160–2.

One can learn immediately the spirit of the crowd,
And the hearts trembling in war.[67]

I never see this divine description without seeming to see human ineptitude and vanity depicted there. For these warlike movements, which
ravish us by their horror and dreadfulness, this tempest of sounds and
cries—

<Here a gleam rises to the sky,
The whole earth is dazzled by the billowing brass.
The sound from their feet is stirred by the force of the men,
    and the mountains,
Struck by its clamor, re-echo it to the stars>[68]

—this terrible array of some many thousands of armed men, full of fury,
ardor, and courage: it is pleasant to consider by how many foolish
causes it is excited and by what lightweight causes it is extinguished.

They tell us it was because of the love of Paris
That Greece and the land of barbarians came into such
    conflict.[69]

All Asia was lost and consumed in wars for Paris' lechery. One single
man's desire, a case of spite, of pleasure, of domestic jealousy—causes
that would not move two fishwives to scratch one another—this is the
soul and the moving force of all this great trouble. Are we to believe those
who are their principal authors and movers? Let us listen to the greatest,
the most victorious Emperor, the most powerful who ever was, disporting
himself and making laughable, most comically and cleverly, numerous
battles hazarded by sea and by land, the blood and the life of five hundred thousand men who followed his fortune, and the forces and riches
of two parts of the world exhausted in the service of his undertakings:

As Antony made love to Glaphyra, my duty,
According to Fulvia, is to make love to Fulvia.
Shall I make love to Fulvia? And what if Manius
Wants me to commit an unnatural act with him? I think not,
    if I am wise.

67. Virgil, *Georgics*, IV, 67–9.
68. Lucretius, *De rerum natura*, II, 325–8.
69. Horace, *Epistles*, I, ii, 6.

Make love or do battle, she says? Indeed! What if my member
Is dearer to me than life itself? Let the trumpets sound![70]

(I use my Latin in freedom of conscience, with the permission you have given me.) Now this great body, with so many faces and movements, which seems to menace the heavens and the earth:

<*Like the waves rolling on the Libyan sea,*
When fierce Orion plunges into the wintry waves,
When, at the new sun, the thick ears are scorched,
In the vale of Hermus, or in the yellowing fields of Lycia,
The shields ring, and the ground trembles, stirred up by the
    striking of the feet.>[71]

This furious monster with so many arms and so many heads is always feeble, calamitous, and wretched man. It is only an anthill stirred up and heated:

The black battle line moves across the plain.[72]

A contrary gust of wind, the croaking of a flight of crows, a horse's false step, the accidental passing of an eagle, a dream, a voice, a sign, a morning mist suffice to overturn the monster and bring it to the ground. Just give it a ray of sun on its face—there it is, melted and fainting; just let someone blow a little dust in its eyes, like our poet's honeybees—there are all our colors, our legions, and the great Pompey himself at their head, broken and jumbled: for it was he, it seems to me, whom Sertorius defeated in Spain with these fine weapons <which have also served others, like Eumenes against Antigonus or Surena against Crassus>:

These movements of souls and these great battles
Will grow calm, held in check when dust is thrown at them.[73]

<<If you let loose even some of our flies, they will have both the power and the courage to disperse the horde. In recent memory, when

---

70. Martial, *Epigrams*, XI, xxi, 3–8; Martial attributes the verse to Augustus.
71. Virgil, *Aeneid*, VII, 718–22.
72. Virgil, *Georgics*, IV, 404.
73. Virgil, *Georgics*, IV, 86–7.

the Portuguese were besieging the city of Tamly in the territory of Xia-time, the inhabitants of that place brought to the wall a great quantity of hives, in which they were rich. And with fire they drove the bees so fiercely at their enemies, that they were put to rout, since they could not support their attacks and their stings. Thus the victory and the freedom of their city was due to this new form of relief, with such success that, at their return from combat, not a single bee was reported missing.>>

The souls of Emperors and of cobblers are cast in the same mold. Considering the importance of the actions of princes, and their weight, we persuade ourselves that they are produced by some causes just as weighty and important. We are deceiving ourselves: they are pushed and pulled in their movements by the same mechanism that we are in our own. The same reason that makes us tangle with a neighbor, between Princes, starts a war; the same reason that makes us whip a lackey, when it happens in a King, makes him ruin a province. <Their wishes are as frivolous as ours, but they can do more.> Like appetites agitate a mite and an elephant.

As to loyalty, there is no animal in the world as treacherous as man. Our histories recount the lively pursuit that some dogs have made after the deaths of their masters. King Pyrrhus, who had encountered a dog guarding a dead man and had heard that it had been doing this for three days, ordered the body to be buried and took the dog along with him. One day when he was present at the general review of his army, this dog, seeing its master's murderers, ran after them with great barks and fierce anger and by this indication set in motion vengeance for this murder, which was soon accomplished in the path of justice. The sage Hesiod's dog did as much, when it convicted the children of Ganistor (from Naupactus) of the murder committed on the person of its master. Another dog, on guard at a temple in Athens, when it saw a sacrilegious thief carrying off the most beautiful jewels, began to bark at him as hard as it could; but when the wardens did not wake at the noise, it began to follow the thief, and when daylight came, it kept a little way off without losing sight of him. If he offered it food, it would have none of it, while it wagged its tail at other passersby whom it encountered on its way and took from their hands whatever they gave it to eat. If its thief stopped to sleep, it stopped too, in the same place. When news of this dog came to the wardens of that church, they set out to follow in its tracks, asking for news of a dog with that appearance, and they finally found it in the city of Cromyon, and the thief too, whom they brought back to the city of Athens where he was punished. And the judges, in recognition of this good deed, ordered, at public expense, a certain measure of wheat to feed the dog, and ordered the priests to take care of it. Plutarch testifies to this story as something well-attested to that happened in his own century.

As for gratitude (for it seems to me that we need to bring that word into favor) this single example will suffice, of which Apion reports, having himself been an eyewitness. One day, he says, when the people at Rome were being given the pleasure of the combat of many strange beasts, and chiefly of lions of unusual size, there was among them one who, by his furious mien, by the power and size of his limbs, and by a proud and terrible roar, attracted the attention of the whole audience. Among the slaves who were presented to the people in combat with these beasts was one Androdus of Dacia, who belonged to a Roman lord of consular rank. This lion, seeing him from a distance, first stopped short, as if struck with wonder, and then approached him quite gently, in a soft and peaceful manner, as if it were going to acknowledge him. This done, and when it had been assured of what it was looking for, it began to wag its tail in the manner of dogs making up to their master and to kiss and lick the hands and thighs of this poor wretch who was transfixed with terror and beside himself. When Androdus had recovered his spirits, thanks to the benevolence of this lion, and regained his vision sufficiently to look at it and recognize it, it was a singular pleasure to see the caresses and the greetings that they exchanged with one another. At this the people rose with cries of joy, and the Emperor had the slave summoned to hear from him the reason for so strange an event. He recounted to him a novel and amazing history:

"When my master was proconsul in Africa," he said, "I was forced by the cruelty and rigor with which he treated me—he had me beaten every day—to steal off and run away. And to hide safely from someone with such great power in the province, I found my quickest way was to seek out the deserts, the sandy and uninhabitable districts of that country, resolved, if means of sustenance should fail me, to find some way of killing myself. Since the sun was extremely harsh and the heat insupportable at noon, when I came on a hidden and inaccessible cave I threw myself into it. Soon thereafter this lion arrived with a bleeding and wounded paw, complaining and groaning at the pain it was suffering. At its arrival, I was sorely afraid; but the lion, seeing me cringing in a corner of its lair, came gently up to me, presenting its injured paw, showing it to me as if to ask for help. I then removed a large splinter that was in it, and now that I was somewhat used to the lion, squeezed the wound, extracting the pus that had accumulated in it, dried it, and cleaned it as well as I could. The lion, feeling itself relieved of its suffering and eased of its pain, lay down to rest and to sleep, all the time keeping its paw between my hands. From then on, the lion and I lived

together in that cave for three whole years, on the same food; for of the
beasts that it killed in the hunt, it always brought me the best pieces,
which, for lack of fire, I cooked in the sun and lived on. Finally, weary-
ing of this brutal and savage life, one day when this lion was away on its
usual quest, I left there, and, on the third day, was surprised by soldiers,
who took me from Africa to this city, to my master, who at once condemned me to death and to be thrown to the beasts. But, as I see, this
lion was also captured soon thereafter and now wishes to repay me for
the favor and the cure it received from me."

This is the story that Androdus told the Emperor, which he also
recounted to the people here and there. So, at the request of all, he was
set free and absolved of his sentence, and by order of the people was
made a present of that lion. Since then, says Apion, we see Androdus
leading that lion on a very small leash, strolling among the taverns of
Rome, receiving the money that is given him, while the lion allows
itself to be covered with the flowers thrown at it, while everyone who
meets them says, "There is the lion, host to the man; there is the man,
physician to the lion."

<We often weep at the loss of beasts that we love, as they do ours:

> *Then his warhorse, Ethon, without adornments, goes crying,*
> *His brow moist with great tears.*[74]

As some of our nations have their wives in common, and others each
his own, is that not also seen among the beasts? Do they not also have
marriages better kept than ours?>

As for the society and confederation that animals arrange among
themselves to unite and assist one another, it may be observed of cattle,
of swine and other animals, that, at the cry of the one you are injuring,
the whole troop runs to its assistance and rallies to its defense. When
the parrot fish has swallowed the fisherman's bait, its comrades gather
in a crowd around it and gnaw the line; and if by chance there is one of
them who had gotten into the net, the others offer it their tail from outside, and it grips the tail tightly with its teeth; thus they pull it out and
get it away. Barbels, when one of their comrades is caught, put the line
against their backs, raising a spine they have that is toothed like a saw,
with which they saw and cut it.

As to the particular duties we perform for one another in the service
of life, we see many similar examples among animals. They hold that
the whale never moves unless it has in front of it a little fish like a sea

74. Virgil, *Aeneid*, XI, 89–90.

gudgeon, which is therefore called the guide-fish; the whale follows it, letting itself be led and turned as easily as the tiller turns the ship; and, in recompense, again, while everything else, whether beast or vessel, that enters into the horrible chaos of the mouth of that monster is incontinently lost and swallowed up, this little fish retires there with complete security and sleeps there, and during its sleep the whale never budges; but as soon as it comes out, the whale starts to follow it without stopping; and if it happens to lose the fish, the whale goes wandering here and there, sometimes bruising itself against the rocks, like a vessel that has no rudder, something that Plutarch testifies to having seen at the island of Anticyra.

There is a similar association between the little bird called the wren and the crocodile. The wren serves as sentinel for that large animal; and if its enemy, the ichneumon, approaches to fight it, for fear it might be surprised in its sleep, this little bird starts its song and, by pecking the crocodile with its beak, wakes it and warns it of its danger. The wren lives on the leavings of this monster, who receives it comfortably in its mouth and allows it to peck in its jaws and between its teeth; and if it wants to close its mouth, it first advises the wren to leave, closing its mouth little by little, without squeezing or injuring the bird.

The shellfish called the nacre also lives in the same way with the pinnothere, which is a little animal like a crab that serves it as usher and doorman, sitting at the mouth of that shellfish, which it constantly holds ajar and open, until it sees entering some little fish suitable for their prey; for then the pinnothere enters the nacre, pinching its live flesh and making it close its shell. Then together they both eat the prey confined in their fort.

In the way tuna fish live, we notice a remarkable knowledge of three parts of mathematics. As to astrology, they teach it to man; for they stop at the place where the winter solstice overtakes them and do not stir from there until the following equinox; that is why even Aristotle willingly acknowledges that they possess this science. As for geometry and arithmetic, they always form their school in a cubic shape, square in every direction, and arrange it into a solid battalion, closed and surrounded on all sides with six surfaces all equal; then they swim in this square formation, as wide in the rear as in front, so that whoever sees and counts one side can easily number the whole troop, since the number in depth is equal to the width, and the width to the length.

As to high-mindedness, it is hard to offer a clearer image of it than the case of the big dog that was sent to King Alexander from the Indies. It was first presented with a deer to fight, and then a boar, and then a bear; it took no account of them and did not deign to stir from its place.

But when the dog saw a lion, it at once rose to his feet, clearly showing that it thought this one worthy of entering into combat with.

<As to repentance and regret for faults committed, we are told of an elephant who, when it had killed its keeper in a fit of anger, felt such extreme grief that it would never again eat anything and allowed itself to die.>

As for clemency, it is told of a tiger, the most inhuman beast of all, that when a young goat was given it, it suffered two days of hunger before it would injure the goat, and on the third day it broke the cage where it was confined, to go and look for other food, not wanting to attack the goat, its friend and its guest.

And as to the rights of familiarity and understanding that are produced by association, it happens to us quite ordinarily that we bring cats, dogs, and hares to live together. But what experience teaches those who travel by sea, and especially on the sea of Sicily, about the condition of the kingfisher surpasses all human thought. What species of animal has nature ever so honored in its confinement, birth, and delivery? For the poets do say that one single island of Delos, which was formerly floating, was made firm to serve the delivery of Latona; but God wished the whole sea to be stopped and made smooth and calm, without waves, without winds, and without rain, while the kingfisher produces its little ones, which is just about at the solstice, the shortest day of the year; and, because it is so favored, we have seven days and seven nights in the very heart of winter when we can navigate without danger. Their females acknowledge no other male but their own and accompany him all their life without leaving him; if he becomes weakened and broken, they put him up on their shoulders, carry him everywhere, and serve him until death. But no competence has yet been able to arrive at the knowledge of that marvelous manufacture by which the kingfisher composes the nest for her little ones, nor can anyone guess its material. Plutarch, who has seen and handled a number of them, thinks that they are the bones of some fish, which she joins and pulls together, interlacing them, some lengthwise, others crosswise, and adding curves and loops, so that at last she forms from them a vessel quite ready to sail; then, when she has finished building it, she carries it to the pulsing tide, where the sea, beating it gently, shows her how to repair what is not well-joined and to reinforce the places where she sees that the structure is loosening and coming apart under the blows of the sea; and, on the contrary, you will find the beating of the sea strengthens and tightens what is well-joined, so that it can neither break, nor dissolve, nor be damaged by blows of stone or iron except with great difficulty. And what is even more to be admired is the proportion and shape of the internal space; for it is composed and proportioned in such a way that it can admit nothing except the bird that has built it; for to any other thing it is impenetrable, tight, and closed, so that nothing can enter, not even the sea water. This is a very clear description of that edifice, borrowed from a good source; nevertheless it seems to me that it does not make clear enough to us the difficulty of that architecture. Now from what vanity can it come about that we place beneath us, and interpret disdainfully, actions that we can neither imitate nor understand?

To pursue a little further this equality and correspondence that we have with the beasts: the privilege with which our soul glorifies itself, of reducing to its condition everything it conceives, of stripping of mortal and corporeal qualities all that belongs to it, of ordering all the things it deems worthy of its acquaintance to relinquish and divest themselves of their corruptible conditions and making them leave aside like vile and superfluous vestments their thickness, length, depth, weight, color, smell, roughness, smoothness, hardness, softness, and all sensible accidents, in order to accommodate them to its immortal and spiritual condition, so that the Rome and Paris I have in my soul, Paris that I imagine, I imagine and I comprehend without magnitude and without place, without stone, without plaster, and without wood—this same privilege, I say, seems very evidently to belong to the beasts; for a horse, accustomed to trumpets, to the firing of muskets, and to battles, which we see trembling and shaking in its sleep, stretched out on its litter, as if it were in the thick of the fight: it is certain that in its soul it is conceiving the sound of a drum that makes no noise, an army without arms or body:

> We see strong horses, stretched out in sleep,
> Sweating so much, and often sighing,
> As if putting out all their strength in contention for a prize.[75]

This hare that a greyhound imagines in its sleep, after which we see it panting while asleep, stretching out its tail, shaking its legs, and representing perfectly the movements of the chase, is a hare without skin or bones:

> Hunting dogs often, in the course of a gentle sleep,
> Suddenly shake their legs: they bark,
> Sniff around themselves with sudden thrusts,
> As if they were tracking down and following the game,

75. Lucretius, *De rerum natura*, IV, 988–90.

Or they start up, following the empty simulacra of deer,
As if they saw them running away;
Until the error is dispelled, and they come to their senses.[76]

The watchdogs we often see growl while dreaming and then bark out-right and wake themselves up with a start, as if they saw some stranger coming: that stranger that their soul sees is a spiritual and imperceptible man, without dimensions, without color, and without being:

. . . see the gentle house dogs grow excited,
Wipe a bit of sleep from their eyes,
And rise from the ground with a leap, thinking they see
Unknown visages and faces.[77]

As to bodily beauty, before we go any further, I must know if we are agreed about its description. We probably do not know what beauty is in nature and in general, since we give so many different forms to our human beauty. <<If there were some natural prescription for it, we would recognize it in common, like the heat of the fire. We imagine its forms as we like.>>

<A Belgian color is ugly on a Roman face.>[78]

The Indies paint it black and swarthy, with large swollen lips, and a big flat nose. <And they load the cartilage between the nostrils with heavy gold rings to make it hang down to the mouth, as also the lower lip with great hoops enriched with precious stones, so that it hangs down to their chin; and it is their fashion to show their teeth down to the base of the roots. In Peru the largest ears are the most beautiful, and they extend them artificially as far as they can: <<and a man of today says he has seen in one eastern nation this care for enlarging the ears and loading them with heavy jewels so much in fashion that he would pass his arm, with its clothing, through a hole in an ear.>> There are nations elsewhere that blacken their teeth with great care and dislike seeing them white; in other places, they paint them a red color. <<It is not only in the Basque country that women think themselves more beautiful with their heads shaved, but also elsewhere, and what is more,

76. Lucretius, *De rerum natura,* V, 992–8.
77. Lucretius, *De rerum natura,* V, 999–1002.
78. Propertius, *Poems,* II, xviii, 26.

in certain glacial countries, as Pliny says.>> The Mexicans count among beauties the small size of the forehead, and while they trim their hair on all the rest of the body, on the forehead they cultivate it and increase it by artifice, and they have such esteem for large breasts that they affect to be able to suckle their babies over their shoulder. We would represent ugliness that way. The Italians make beauty plump and massive; the Spanish, hollow and gaunt; and among us one makes it fair, the other dark; one soft and delicate, the other strong and vigorous; one demands here daintiness and sweetness, another pride and majesty.> <<Just so do the Epicureans give the preference in beauty, which Plato attributes to the spherical, to the pyramidal or the square, and they cannot swallow a god in the shape of a ball.>>

But, however that may be, nature has no more privileged us in this above her common laws than in the rest. And if we judge ourselves correctly, we shall find that if there are some animals less favored in this than us, there are others, and in great number, who are more so; <<"*we are outdone by many animals in beauty*,"[79] even among the terrestrial animals, our compatriots; for as to sea dwellers (apart from figure, which is so different that it cannot be compared), in color, cleanliness, polish, arrangement, we yield to them completely, and not less, in all qualities, to those of the air. And>> that prerogative that the poets make much of in our upright posture, looking to heaven as its origin—

> *While other animals, prone, look at the earth,*
> *To man he gave an uplifted face, and ordered him*
> *To see the sky and turn his eyes up to the stars*[80]

—this is truly poetic, for there are numerous little beasts whose sight is turned entirely to the sky, and I find the appearance of the necks of camels and ostriches even more elevated and straighter than ours.

<<What animals fail to have their face above and at the front, to look at one another as we do, and to discover in their proper posture as much of the sky and the earth as man does?

And what qualities of our bodily constitution, as described in Plato and in Cicero, cannot serve a thousand kinds of beasts?>>

The animals that resemble us most are the ugliest and most abject of the whole crowd; for in external appearance and facial form, the ones closest to us are the Barbary apes—

79. Seneca, *Epistles*, CXXIV.
80. Ovid, *Metamorphoses*, I, 84.

<<*How like are the apes, the ugliest beasts, to us!*>>[81]

—for the interior and the vital parts, the closest is the pig. Indeed, when I imagine man quite naked (even in that sex that seems to have the greater share of beauty), his blemishes, his natural weakness, and his imperfections, I find that we have more reason than any other animal to cover ourselves. It was excusable of us to borrow from those nature has favored more than us, to adorn ourselves with their beauty and to hide under what they cast off—wool, feathers, fur, silk.

Notice moreover that we are the only animal whose shortcomings offend our own companions and the only one who has to hide, in our natural actions, from our own species. Truly it is a circumstance worthy of consideration that the masters of the art recommend as a cure for the amorous passions the complete and unimpeded sight of the body being pursued, and that, to cool love, all that is needed is to see freely what we love:

> *He has seen the obscene parts of a body offered him,*
> *And love collapses in the midst of this pursuit.*[82]

And although this prescription may perhaps stem from a somewhat delicate and frigid disposition, still it is a wonderful sign of our weakness that habit and familiarity disgust us with one another. <It is not so much modesty as art and prudence that make our ladies so circumspect in refusing us an entrance to their boudoirs before they are painted and ready to show themselves publicly:>

> *Nor are our mistresses ignorant of this:*
> *Wherefore they carefully hide everything behind the*
>   *backdrop of their life,*
> *Away from those they wish to keep firmly entangled and*
>   *bound in love.*[83]

Yet in numerous animals there is nothing of theirs that we do not love and that does not please our senses, so that even from their excrement and their discharge we obtain not only dainty morsels to eat but also our richest ornaments and perfumes.

81. Ennius, cited by Cicero, *De natura deorum*, I, xxxv.
82. Ovid, *Remedia amoris*, 429–30.
83. Lucretius, *De rerum natura*, IV, 1182–4.

This argument concerns only our common order and is not so sacrilegious as to want to include those divine, supernatural, and extraordinary beauties that we sometimes see shining among us like stars under a corporeal and terrestrial veil.

What is more, the very part of the favors of nature that we allow to the animals is, by our own confession, most advantageous to them. We attribute to ourselves imaginary and fantastic goods, future and absent goods, for which human capacity by itself cannot answer, or goods that we falsely attribute to ourselves through our ungoverned opinion, such as reason, knowledge, and honor; and to them we leave as their portion goods that are essential, palpable, and tangible: peace, repose, security, innocence, and health—health, I say, the fairest and the richest gift that nature can bestow upon us. Thus philosophy, in the case of Stoicism, dares to say that Heraclitus and Pherecydes would have done well if they could have exchanged their wisdom for health and freed themselves of the illnesses, the one of hydropsy, the other of the affliction of lice, that oppressed them. In this way, they give yet more weight to wisdom, comparing it with and balancing it against health, than they do in any other proposition that is theirs. They say that if Circe had presented Ulysses with two beverages, one to make a foolish man wise and the other, a wise man foolish, Ulysses would have done better to accept that of folly than to consent to Circe's changing his human shape to that of a beast; and they say that wisdom itself would have spoken to him in this manner: "Leave me, let me be, rather than house me in the shape and body of an ass." What? Do the philosophers then forsake that great and divine wisdom for this corporeal and terrestrial veil? So it is not through reason, through discourse and through the soul that we excel the beasts; it is through our beauty, our fair skin, and the lovely disposition of our limbs, for which we must abandon our intelligence, our prudence, and all the rest.

Now I accept this naïve and frank confession. Certainly, philosophers knew that those attributes about which we make such a to-do are only a vain fantasy. If the beasts had all the Stoic virtue, knowledge, wisdom, and self-sufficiency, they would still be beasts; nor would they be therefore comparable to a wretched, nasty, and senseless man. <<Finally, everything not the way we are is worth nothing. And God himself, if he is to be valued, must resemble man, as we shall say in a moment. Thus it appears>> that it is not through true discourse, but through a foolish and opinionated pride, that we prefer ourselves to the other animals and cut ourselves off from their condition and their society.

[3. Man's Knowledge Cannot Make Him Happy]

But to return to my subject, we have, for our part, inconstancy, irresolution, incertitude, grief, superstition, concern about things to come, even after our life, ambition, avarice, jealousy, envy, appetites that are unruly, mad, and uncontrollable, war, falsehood, disloyalty, disparagement, and curiosity. Certainly, we have strangely overpaid for this fine rationality we boast of and this capacity to judge and to know, if we have bought it at the price of that infinite number of passions in which we are constantly entangled. <Unless we want to set great store, as Socrates surely did,[84] on this remarkable prerogative over other animals, that while nature has set them certain seasons and limits to sexual pleasures, she has given us free rein at all hours and on all occasions.> <<"As with wine for sick men, since it is rarely good for them, but often harmful, it is better to give them none at all than to expose them to certain injury for the sake of a doubtful cure; in the same way I do not know whether it would perhaps be better for mankind if nature had refused it that activity of thought, that penetration, that industry we call reason, which she has granted us so liberally and so broadly, since that activity is salutary only for a small number and is harmful to all the rest."*>>[85]

What good can we suppose that knowledge of so many things was to Varro and Aristotle? Did it exempt them from human discomforts? Were they immune to the accidents that afflict a porter? Did they derive from logic some consolation for the gout? Because they knew how that humor lodges in the joints, did they feel it any less? Were they reconciled to death because they knew that some countries rejoice in it, or to cuckoldry because they knew that in some regions wives are held in common? On the contrary, although they held the first rank in knowledge—the one among the Romans, the other among the Greeks—and at the time when knowledge was at its peak, still we have not heard that they had any particular excellence in their life; indeed, the Greek had his work cut out for him to clear some noticeable stains in his.

<Has it been found that sensual pleasure and health are more enjoyable for those who know astrology and grammar?

Well, does the illiterate's organ stand less erect?[86]

And are shame and poverty less oppressive?

84. Xenophon, *Memorabilia*, I, iv, 12.
85. Cicero, *De natura deorum*, III, xxvii.
86. Horace, *Epodes*, VIII, 17.

Clearly you will miss sickness and debility,
And you will escape affliction and care, and long years of life
Will be given you with a better destiny.[87]

In my time, I have seen a hundred artisans, a hundred laborers, wiser and happier than university rectors and whom I would prefer to resemble. Learning—this is my opinion—ranks among things necessary to life, like honor, nobility, dignity, <<or further, like beauty, riches,>> and such other qualities as do in fact serve it but from a distance and a bit more through fancy than through nature.>

<<We need hardly more duties, rules, and laws for living in our community than the cranes and ants in theirs. And despite this, we see that they conduct themselves in a very orderly way without learning. If man were wise, he would fix the true price of each thing according to its greatest utility and fitness for his life.>>

Whoever rates us by our actions and behavior will find a much greater number of excellent people among the ignorant than among the learned: I say in every sort of virtue. The old Rome seems to me to have supported men of greater worth, both for peace and for war, than that learned Rome that ruined itself. Even if the rest were exactly equal, at least integrity and innocence would remain on the side of the old, for it dwells particularly well with simplicity.

But I leave this argument, which would take me much farther than I would wish to follow. I will add simply that it is only humility and submission that can produce a good man. The knowledge of his duty must not be left to each one's judgment. It must be prescribed for him. He must not be allowed to choose according to his reasoning; otherwise, according to the imbecility and infinite variety of our arguments and opinions, we would finally forge for ourselves duties that would set us to eating one another, as Epicurus says. The first law that God ever gave man was a law of pure obedience. It was a bare and simple commandment in which man had nothing to know or to chat about; <<thus, to obey is the chief duty of a reasonable soul, recognizing a heavenly overlord and benefactor. From obeying and yielding springs every other virtue, as every sin arises from being opinionated.>> <And on the other hand, the first temptation that came to human nature from the side of the devil, his first poison, was insinuated in us through the promises he made us of knowledge and awareness: *"You will be like gods, knowing good and evil."*>[88] <<And in Homer the sirens, to trick Ulysses and to

---

87. Juvenal, *Satires*, XIV, 156–8.
88. Genesis 3:5.

draw him into their dangerous and ruinous trap, offered him a gift of knowledge.>>[89] Man's plague is the belief that he has knowledge. That is why ignorance is so highly recommended by our religion as appropriate for belief and obedience. <<*"Beware lest they deceive you through philosophy and vain seductions according to the rudiments of the world."*>>[90]

On this there is general agreement among the philosophers of all sects: that the sovereign good consists in the tranquillity of soul and body. <But where do we find it?>

> *Thus the wise man is below none but Jove,*
> *In short, rich, free, honored, handsome, king of kings, finally*
> *Flourishing in health, except when he has a cold.*[91]

It seems in truth that nature, for the consolation of our miserable and sickly state, has given us for our share only presumption. This is what Epictetus says: that man has nothing uniquely his own except the use of his opinions. We have as our share only wind and smoke. <The gods have health essentially, says philosophy, and sickness in thought; man, on the contrary, possesses his good in imagination, his evils essentially.> We were right in valuing the powers of our imagination, for all our goods are only in our dreams. Hear this poor, calamitous animal boast: "There is nothing," says Cicero, "so sweet as the occupation of letters, of those letters, I say, by means of which the infinity of things, the immense grandeur of nature, the heavens of this very world, and the lands and the seas are opened to us; it is they that have taught us religion, moderation, the greatness of courage, and have snatched our soul from the shadows to make it see all things, high, low, first, last, and intermediate; it is they that furnish us the means to live well and happily, and guide us to survive our age without displeasure and without offense." Does he not seem to be speaking of the condition of God, ever-living and all-powerful?

And in fact, a thousand little women in the village have lived an equable life, sweeter and more constant than his:

> *A god, it was a god, great Memmius,*
> *Who first gave us that rule we call wisdom,*
> *And who, by his method,*

89. Homer, *Odyssey*, XII, 188.
90. Colossians 2:8.
91. Horace, *Epistles*, I, i, 106–8.

> Snatching our life from such great storms and darkness,
> Set it in so calm and clear a light.[92]

Those are most magnificent and beautiful words, but a very slight accident puts his intelligence into a worse state than that of the humblest shepherd, despite that instructive God and that divine wisdom. Equally impudent is <<this promise of Democritus' book: "I am going to speak of all things," and that stupid title Aristotle confers on us of mortal Gods; and>> the judgment of Chrysippus that Dion would be as virtuous as God. And my Seneca recognized, he said, that God has given him life, but living well he has from himself, <<in conformity with that other saying: "It is right that we should glory in virtue, which would not happen if we had it as a gift from God and not from ourselves."[93] This is also from Seneca: The sage has courage like God's, but in human frailty, so that his courage surpasses God's.>> There is nothing so common as to meet cases of similar temerity. There is no one of us who is as much offended by seeing himself compared to God as he is at seeing himself abased to the rank of other animals; so much more jealous are we of our own interest than of that of our creator.

But we must trample underfoot this stupid vanity and shake briskly and boldly the absurd foundations on which these false opinions are built. As long as he thinks he has some means and some power of his own, man will never recognize what he owes to his master; he will always make chickens of his eggs, as they say; he must be stripped down to his shirt.

Let us look at a notable example of the effect of his philosophy:

Posidonius, oppressed by an illness so painful that it made him twist his arms and gnash his teeth, thought he was thumbing his nose at the pain by crying out against it: "Do what you like, I still refuse to say that you are bad." He feels the same passions as my lackey, but he prides himself on restraining at least his tongue according to the laws of his sect.

> <<It was wrong to submit in fact while glorying in words.[94]

Arcesilaus was ill with gout, and when Carneades had come to see him and was going away very sorry, Arcesilaus recalled his visitor and showing him his feet and his chest, he said: "Nothing has come from

---

92. Lucretius, *De rerum natura*, V, 8–12.
93. Cicero, *De natura deorum*, III, xxxvi.
94. Cicero, *Tusculan Disputations*, II, xiii.

there to here." At least Arcesilaus has a better grace than Posidonius, for he is aware that he is in pain and would like to be freed of it; but all the same his heart is not beaten down and enfeebled by this evil. The former holds himself in his rigidity, more, I fear, verbal than real. And Dionysius of Heraclea, afflicted with a violent smarting of the eyes, was forced to abandon those Stoic resolutions.>>

But what if knowledge could in fact do what they say, soften and diminish the sharpness of the misfortunes that pursue us, what does it do but what ignorance does much more purely and more evidently? The philosopher Pyrrho, running the risk of a great storm at sea, could offer to those who were with him nothing better to imitate than the serenity of a pig that was traveling with them and looking at that tempest without fear. Philosophy, at the end of its precepts, returns us to the example of an athlete or a mule driver, in whom we ordinarily see much less apprehension of death, pain, or other discomforts, and much more firmness than knowledge ever furnished to anyone who had not been born and prepared for it on his own through a natural disposition. Why can we trim and cut the tender limbs of an infant more easily than ours, if it is not from ignorance? <<And those of a horse?>> How many people has the mere strength of imagination made ill? We see them commonly having themselves bled, purged, and medicated to cure ills that they do not feel except in their thoughts. When real evils fail us, knowledge lends us its own. This color and this complexion foretell for us some catarrhal inflammation; this hot weather threatens us with a feverish feeling; this break in the life line of your left hand advises you of some remarkable impending indisposition. And finally knowledge unblushingly addresses health itself. This lightness and vigor of youth cannot stay in one position; it must be bled and weakened for fear of its turning against itself. Compare the life of a man enslaved by such imaginings with that of a laborer who lets himself go according to his natural appetite, measuring things only by his present feeling, without knowledge and without prognostication, who has no pain except when he has it, while the other often has the stone in his soul before he has it in his kidneys; as if he had not enough time to suffer the pain when he has it, he anticipates it in his fancy and runs to meet it.

Through examples, what I say of medicine can be extended generally to all knowledge. From this has arisen the old opinion of the philosophers that the sovereign good consists in the recognition of the weakness of our judgment. My ignorance gives me as much occasion for hope as for fear, and having no rule for my health except that of the examples of others and of the events that I see elsewhere on similar occasions, I find cases of all sorts and stop with the comparisons that are most favorable to me. I receive health with open arms, free, whole, and complete, and whet my appetite to enjoy it, so much the more so as it is for me at present less ordinary and rarer; so far am I from troubling my repose and its sweetness with the bitterness of a new and constrained form of life. The beasts show us the extent to which the agitation of our minds brings us diseases.

<<What they tell us of the people of Brazil, who die only of old age, a fact that is attributed to the serenity and tranquillity of their air, I attribute instead to the tranquillity and serenity of their souls, freed of any tense or unpleasant passion or thought, like people who would pass their lives in an admirable simplicity and ignorance, without letters, without law, without a king, without any religion.>>

And what explains what we see from experience, that the grossest and most ungainly men are the sturdiest and most desirable in acts of love, and that the love of a mule driver often becomes more acceptable than that of a fine gentleman, if not the fact that in the latter the agitation of his soul disturbs his physical power, breaks it, and exhausts it?

In the same way the soul also commonly exhausts and troubles itself. What drives it mad, what most frequently throws it into lunacy but its quickness, its sharpness, its agility, and, indeed, its own power? <In what does the subtlest madness consist but in the subtlest wisdom? As the greatest enmities arise from the greatest friendships, as mortal diseases arise from the most flourishing states of health, so do the most outstanding and wildest manias arise from the rare and lively agitations of our souls. It takes only a half turn of a pin to pass from one to the other.> From the actions of madmen we see how closely insanity is linked to the most vigorous operations of our souls. Who does not know how imperceptible is the proximity of lunacy to the lively elevations of a free mind and the consequences of a supreme and extraordinary virtue? Plato calls melancholics more teachable and excellent; at the same time there are none who have as great a propensity to madness. Countless minds find themselves ruined by their own power and flexibility. What leap has just been taken, through his own agitation and buoyancy, by one of the most judicious and ingenious men, better instructed in the light of that antique pure poetry than any other Italian poet has been for a long time? Is he not grateful to that murderous vivacity of his, to the clarity that has blinded him, to that exact and tender apprehension of reason that has left him without reason, to that curious and industrious quest for knowledge that has brought him to stupidity, to that rare aptitude for the practices of the mind that has left him without practice and without mind? I felt more anger than compassion on seeing him at Ferrara in his piteous state, surviving himself, ignorant of himself and his works, which without his knowledge, and yet before his eyes, have seen the light uncorrected and shapeless.

Do you want a man healthy, do you want him well-disciplined and in a firm and secure position? Deck him out in darkness, idleness, and lethargy. <<We have to be made into animals in order to become wise, and dazzled in order to be guided.>>

And if you tell me that the advantage of having a cold, blunt sense of pain and evil brings with it the disadvantage of making us also, in consequence, less keen and less fond of the enjoyment of goods and pleasures, that is true; but the misery of our condition means that we have less to enjoy than to flee from, and that the most extreme sensual pleasure moves us less than a slight pain. <<*"Men feel goods more sluggishly than evils."*>>[95] We do not feel the entirety of health as we do the least of maladies:

> *The slightest irritation of the skin affects us,*
> *While being well moves us not at all.*
> *We are happy not to have gout or pleurisy.*
> *We hardly recognize our own health or sense that we are*
>   *well.*[96]

Our well-being is only the privation of being ill. That is why the philosophical sect that has placed the highest value on sensual pleasure has still ranked it with mere apathy. Not to have anything wrong is to have as much good as man can hope for. <<As Ennius said:

> *There is too much of good for him for whom there is nothing*
>   *wrong.*>>[97]

For that same tickling and stinging that we meet in certain pleasures and that seems to lift us above simple health and apathy, that active, moving, and, I know not how, boiling and biting voluptuousness, even that points only to apathy as its goal. The appetite that drives us to intercourse with women seeks only to chase away the pain that ardent and raging desire brings on us, and demands only that it be assuaged and brought to rest in exemption from that fever. The same holds for other appetites.

95. Livy, *Histories*, XXX, xxi.
96. La Boétie, *Latin Poems*.
97. Cited by Cicero, *De finibus*, II, xiii.

I say, therefore, that if simplicity leads us to have no pain, it leads us to a most happy state according to our condition.

<<Yet we must not imagine that state so leaden that it would be entirely without feeling. For Crantor was right to combat the apathy of Epicurus, if one built it so deeply that even the approach and the birth of evils were not to be perceived. I do not in the least praise that apathy that is neither possible nor desirable. I am contented not to be ill; but, if I am ill, I want to know that I am, and if I am cauterized or incised, I want to feel it. Indeed, he who would uproot the knowledge of evil, would destroy at the same time the recognition of sensual pleasure, and would finally annihilate man: *"This painlessness does not come without a great price, barbarism in the soul, stupor in the body."*[98]

Illness in its turn is good for man. Pain is not always something for him to flee, nor is voluptuousness always to be followed.>>

It is a very great advantage for the honor of ignorance that knowledge itself throws us into its arms when it finds itself prevented from steeling us against the weight of evils; knowledge is constrained to come to this compromise, to give us the reins and allow us to take refuge on the lap of ignorance, and by its favor to protect ourselves from the blows and injuries of fortune. For what else can one say when knowledge instructs us to <<withdraw our thoughts from the evils that grip us, and occupy them with lost pleasures of sense, and>> make use, as consolation for present ills, of the remembrance of past goods, and call to our aid a vanished satisfaction to oppose what now afflicts us: <<*"He places the easing of pain in distraction from thinking of troubles and in turning back to the contemplation of pleasures"*?>>[99] — unless it is the case that where knowledge lacks power it will use cunning and nimble footwork when strength of body and arms fails it. For not only to a philosopher but simply to a well-balanced man, when he in fact feels the burning thirst of a high fever, is the memory of the sweetness of Greek wine the right coin for his recompense? <That would rather make his bargain worse:

For to remember the good doubles the pain.>

Of the same kind is that other advice that philosophy gives, to hold in memory only past happiness, and to erase from it the sorrows we have suffered, as if we had in our power the science of forgetfulness. <<Such advice, moreover, makes us worse.

98. Cicero, *Tusculan Disputations*, III, vi.
99. Cicero, *Tusculan Disputations*, III, xiii.

Sweet is the memory of past troubles.>>[100]

How does philosophy, which ought to put weapons into my hand to combat fortune, which ought to stiffen my courage to trample underfoot all human adversities, come to such weakness as to make me save myself by these cowardly and ridiculous evasions? For memory represents to us not what we choose but what it pleases. Besides, there is nothing that imprints something so vividly in our memory as the desire to forget it; it is a good way of keeping and imprinting something in our soul to beg the soul to lose it. <<And this is false: *"It is in our power, both to bury misfortunes, as it were, in perpetual oblivion, and to remember good fortune with joy and delight."*[101] And this is true: *"For I bear in mind what I do not want to, and I cannot forget what I want to."*>>[102] And whose is this advice? His, <<*"who alone dares to call himself wise,"*>>[103]

> *Who exceeded human kind by his genius,*
> *And dimmed all the stars, as does the rising sun.*[104]

To empty and clear out the memory, is that not the true and proper road to ignorance? <<"Ignorance is a weak remedy for our ills.">>[105] We find a number of similar precepts by which we are allowed to borrow frivolous illusions from the vulgar where lively and strong reason does not avail, provided that they offer us contentment and consolation. Where they cannot cure the wound, they are happy to benumb and weaken it. I believe they will not deny me this, that if they could add order and constancy to a state of life that maintains itself in pleasure and tranquillity by some weakness and malady of judgment, they would accept it:

> *I shall begin to drink and scatter flowers,*
> *Even though I be thought foolish.*[106]

We could find numerous philosophers who agree with Lycas: this man, who was otherwise well-ordered in his behavior, living calmly and

100. Cicero, *De finibus*, I, xvii.
101. Cicero, *De finibus*, I, xvii.
102. Cicero, *De finibus*, II, xxxii.
103. Cicero, *De finibus*, II, iii.
104. Lucretius, *De rerum natura*, III, 1056–7.
105. Seneca, *Oedipus*, III, 17.
106. Horace, *Epistles*, I, v, 14–5.

peacefully in his family, failing in no feature of his duty to his own and to strangers, protecting himself very ably from hurtful things, by some alteration of the senses had an illusion planted in his imagination: he thought he was continually at the theater, watching entertainments, spectacles, and the finest comedies in the world. When doctors cured him of this corrupt humor, he came close to suing them to restore him to the sweetness of his imaginings,

> . . . alas, you have killed me, my friends,
> Not cured me, he said, thus driving away my pleasure,
> And chasing off by force the delightful error of my mind.[107]

His illusion was like that of Thrasilaus, son of Pythodorus, who made himself believe that all the ships leaving and arriving at the port of Piraeus were working only in his service; he rejoiced at the good luck of their navigation and received them with joy. When his brother Crito had him restored to his senses, he missed the kind of condition in which he had been living, full of jollity and free of all sorrow. That is what the old Greek verse says: there is great comfort in not being well-informed—

> In thinking not at all is the sweetest life[108]

—and Ecclesiastes: "In much wisdom there is much grief; and he who increases knowledge, increases travail and sorrow."[109]

There is even that in which philosophy in general agrees, the last prescription it orders for every kind of necessity, to put an end to a life we cannot bear: <<"Does it please you? Bear it. Does it not please you? Get out of it however you can."[110]

"Does pain prick you? Granted even that it tortures you, if you are unprotected, offer it your throat. But if you are protected by the armor of Vulcan, that is, by courage, resist."[111] And there is that saying of convivial Greeks, which they apply here: Aut bibat, aut abeat—Let him drink or leave (it would be more apt in the language of a Gascon, who would be inclined to change the b to a v, rather than in that of Cicero: Aut vivat aut abeat—Let him live or leave):>>

107. Horace, Epistles, II, ii, 138–40.
108. Sophocles, Ajax, 352.
109. Ecclesiastes 1:18.
110. Seneca, Epistles, LXX.
111. Cicero, Tusculan Disputations, II, xiv.

If you do not know how to live properly, leave it to the
   experts;
You have enjoyed enough, eaten and drunk enough;
It is time for you to go, unless properly lusty youth laugh at
   you,
Who have drunk too much wine, and push you aside.[112]

What is all that but a confession of philosophy's impotence and
recourse not only to ignorance for protection, but even to stupidity, to
insensibility and nonexistence?

Democritus, when old age warned him
That the movement of his mind was slowing down,
Aware of the warning, willingly bowed his head to
   approaching death.[113]

This is what Antisthenes said—we should either provide ourselves with
sense to understand or a rope to hang ourselves—and what Chrysippus
quoted on the subject from the poet Tyrtaeus:

Draw near to virtue or to death.[114]

<<And Crates said that love was cured by hunger, if not by time; and
if not by those two means, by the halter.>>
<That Sextius of whom Seneca and Plutarch speak with such high
approval, throwing himself, after abandoning everything, into the study
of philosophy, thought of casting himself into the sea, when he found
the progress of his studies too slow and too long. He ran to meet death
for lack of knowledge. Here are the words of the law on this subject: If
by chance some great misfortune occurs that cannot be remedied, the
port is near, and you can swim out of the body as out of a leaky skiff; for
it is the fear of dying, not the desire to live, that keeps the madman
attached to his body.>

[4. Man's Knowledge Cannot Make Him Good]

As life is made more pleasant by simplicity, so it is also made more
innocent and better, as I was starting to say earlier. "The simple and the

112. Horace, *Epistles*, II, ii, 213–6.
113. Lucretius, *De rerum natura*, III, 1052–4.
114. Plutarch, *Contre les Stoïques* (trans. Amyot), XIV.

ignorant," says Saint Paul, "raise themselves and take hold of heaven, and we, with all our knowledge, plunge ourselves into the infernal abyss." I pause neither at Valentinian, declared enemy of knowledge and letters, nor at Licinius (both Roman emperors), who called them the poison and the plague of every body politic; nor at Mohammed, who <<as I have heard,>> forbade his men to have knowledge. But the example of the great Lycurgus and his authority should certainly have great weight, as should the reverence for that divine Lacedaemonian policy, so great, so admirable, and flourishing for so long a time in virtue and good fortune, without any establishment or exercise of letters. Those who return from that new world that was discovered by the Spanish in our fathers' time can bear witness to us how those nations, without magistrates and without law, live more lawfully and with better regulation than ours, where there are more officers and laws than there are people to be supervised or actions to be regulated:

> *Of citations, requests, examinations,*
> *And papers for power of attorney,*
> *Their hands are full, as well as their pockets —*
> *Commentaries, pieces of advice, and pages in bags,*
> *By which those people prevent the poor devils*
> *From ever having security in their city.*
> *They are besieged front, back, and sideways*
> *By notaries, clerks, and lawyers.*[115]

This is what a Roman senator said of the previous centuries: that their predecessors had their breath stinking of garlic and their stomachs scented with the musk of a clear conscience, and, on the contrary, those of his time smelled only of perfume on the outside, stinking inside with all sorts of vice; that is to say, as I believe, that they had much knowledge and self-conceit and a great lack of integrity. Incivility, ignorance, simplicity, rudeness readily accompany innocence; curiosity, subtlety, knowledge bring malice in their wake; humility, fear, obedience, good nature (which are the chief items for the preservation of human society) demand an empty soul, docile and without self-presumption.

Christians have special knowledge of the extent to which curiosity is a natural and original evil in man. The desire to increase in wisdom and in knowledge: that was the first ruin of mankind; that is the path by which it hurled itself into eternal damnation. Pride is man's downfall

115. Ariosto, *Orlando furioso*, X.

and his corruption; it is pride that throws a man off the common path, that makes him embrace novelties and prefer being chief of an errant troop, committed to following the road to perdition, prefer being regent and preceptor of error and falsehood to being a disciple in the school of truth, allowing himself to be led and guided by another's hand to the beaten path of rectitude. This is perhaps what the ancient Greek maxim says, that superstition follows pride and obeys it as if pride were its father.[116]

<<Oh, pride! How you impede us! When Socrates was told that the god of wisdom had awarded him the title of sage, he was astonished; and, himself examining and searching everywhere, he found no basis for that divine decree. He knew just, temperate, brave people as learned as he was, and more eloquent, handsomer, and more useful to the state. Finally he decided that he was distinguished from the others, and that he was wise, only in that he did not think himself so; that his god thus considered our opinion of our own knowledge and wisdom a stupidity peculiar to mankind, and that our best learning was that of ignorance and our best wisdom, simplicity.>>

Holy Scripture declares miserable those who think well of themselves: "Dust and ashes," it says to them, "what have you to glory in?" And elsewhere: "God has made man like the shadow; who can say of it when it will have vanished with the passing of the light?"[117] In truth we are but nothing. Our powers are so far from conceiving the divine sublimity that, of the works of our creator, those that maximally bear his mark and are maximally his are those we least understand. For Christians it is an occasion to believe if they encounter something unbelievable. The more it is contrary to reason, so much the more is it according to reason. <If it were according to reason, it would no longer be a miracle, and if it were according to some exemplar, it would no longer be unique.> <<"God is better known by not knowing," says Saint Augustine,[118] and Tacitus: "It is holier and more reverent to believe in the works of the gods than to know them."[119]

And Plato holds that there is some vice of impiety in inquiring too curiously of God and the world and of the first causes of things.[120]

---

116. Socrates, from Stobaeus, *Apophthegmata*, sermo 22. Montaigne gives the original Greek after his translation of it.

117. Ecclesiasticus 10:9 and a paraphrase of Ecclesiastes 7:1.

118. Saint Augustine, *De ordine*, II, xvi.

119. Tacitus, *De moribus Germanorum*, xxxiv.

120. Plato, *Laws*, VII, ii.

"*Moreover, it is indeed difficult to find the parent of this universe, and when you have found him, it is wicked to reveal him to the people*," says Cicero.>>[121]

We do indeed say "power," "truth," "justice": those are words that signify something great, but as for the thing itself, we neither see nor conceive it in the least. <We say that God fears, that God is angry, that God loves—

Marking immortal things in mortal words[122]

—these are all agitations and emotions that cannot be lodged in God according to our form, nor can we imagine it according to his.> It is for God alone to know himself and to interpret his works. <<And he does it in our language, improperly, in order to lower himself and descend to us, who are on the ground, prostrate. How can prudence, which is the choice between good and evil, belong to him, seeing that no evil touches him? How can reason and intelligence, of which we make use in order to move from the obscure to the clear, seeing that there is nothing obscure to God? Justice, which distributes to each what belongs to him, devised for the society and community of men: how is it in God? How in God is temperance—the moderation of bodily desires, which have no place in divinity? The courage to bear pain, toil, dangers belong to God just as little, these three things having no access near him. Therefore Aristotle considers God equally exempt from virtue and from vice.

"*He is capable neither of favor nor of anger, since where such passions are, they are all weaknesses.*">>[123]

As for our participation in the knowledge of the truth, such as it is, it is not by our own powers that we have acquired it. God has taught us enough of that through the witnesses he has chosen among the common people, simple and ignorant, to instruct us in his admirable secrets: our faith is not our own acquisition; it is a pure gift of another's liberality. It is not by reasoning or by our intellect that we have received our religion, it is by external authority and commandment. The weakness of our judgment assists us rather than its strength, and our blindness, rather than our clear sight. It is through the mediation of our ignorance rather than of our knowledge that we are knowers of that divine knowledge. It is no marvel that our natural and terrestrial means

121. Quoting Plato, *Timaeus* (trans. Cicero), chapter 2.
122. Lucretius, *De rerum natura*, V, 121.
123. Cicero, *De natura deorum*, I, xvii.

cannot conceive that supernatural and celestial knowledge. Let us bring
to it only our obedience and subjection: "For, as it is written, I shall
destroy the wisdom of the wise, and abase the prudence of the prudent.
Where is the wise man? Where is the scribe? Where is the debater of
this world? Has God not made foolish the wisdom of this world? For,
since the world has never known God through wisdom, it has pleased
him, by the folly of preaching, to save the faithful."[124]

[5. Man Has No Knowledge]

Still I must finally see if it is in man's capacity to find what he is seeking
and if that quest that he has been engaged in for so many centuries has
enriched him with any new powers and any solid truth.

I believe he will admit to me, if he speaks in good conscience, that
all the benefit he has gained from so long a pursuit is to have learned to
recognize his weakness. By long study we have confirmed and verified
the ignorance that was in us by nature. What happens to ears of wheat
happens to really learned men: they go on rising and lifting themselves,
their heads high and proud, as long as they are empty; but in their
maturity, when they are full and swollen with grain, they begin to grow
humble and to hunch over. In the same way, men who have tried everything and probed everything, and have found in that heap of knowledge
and in the provision of so many different things nothing solid and firm
and nothing but vanity, have renounced their presumption and recognized their natural condition.

<<This is what Velleius reproached Cotta and Cicero for, that they
have learned from Philo that they had learned nothing.

Writing to Thales when he was dying, Pherecydes, one of the seven
sages, said: "I have ordered my people, when they have buried me, to
bring you my writings; if they please you and the other sages, publish
them; if not, suppress them; they contain no certainty that is satisfying
to myself. Moreover, I do not profess to know the truth and to attain it; I
open up things rather than discovering them.">> The wisest man there
ever was, when he was asked what he knew, answered that he knew this:
that he knew nothing. He was confirming the saying that the largest
part of what we know is the smallest part of the things we do not know;
that is to say, that even what we think we know is a piece, and a very
small piece, of our ignorance.

<<We know things in a dream, said Plato, and in truth we are igno-
rant of them.

124. 1 Corinthians 1:19–21.

"*Almost all the Ancients said that nothing can be recognized, per-ceived, known, that our senses are limited, our minds imbecilic, the course of our lives short.*">>[125]

Even of Cicero, who owes all his strength to knowledge, Valerius says that in his old age he began to lose esteem for letters. <<And when he treated them, he did so without commitment to any side, following, according to what seemed to him probable, now one sect, now another, thus maintaining at all times the Academy's habit of doubting.

"*I have to speak, but in such a way that I affirm nothing, inquiring into all things, doubting most of them and distrusting myself.*">>[126]

I would have too easy a time if I wanted to consider man in his com-mon state and in general, and yet I could do so by his own rule, which judges truth not by the weight of voices but by their number. Let us leave aside the people

> *Who snore when awake,*
> *For whom life is death, although they live and see,*[127]

who feel nothing, who make no judgments, who leave most of their nat-ural faculties idle. I want to take man in his highest position. Let us consider him in that small number of excellent and chosen men who, gifted with a fine and special natural power, have stiffened and sharp-ened it by care, by study, and by art, and have elevated it to the highest point <<of wisdom>> that it could reach. They have managed their soul in every direction and from every angle; they have supported it and propped it up with all the external help appropriate to it and enriched and ornamented it with all that they could borrow for its advantage from the inside and outside of the world. It is in them that the utmost height of human nature dwells. They have regulated the world of poli-tics and laws; they have instructed it with arts and sciences and instructed it further by the example of their admirable conduct. I shall take into account only those people, their evidence and their experi-ence. Let us see how far they have gone and what they have held. The maladies and defects that we find in this constituency the world will be able boldly to acknowledge as its own.

Whoever seeks anything comes to this point: he says that he has found it, or that he cannot find it, or that he is still looking for it. All of philosophy is divided into these three kinds. Its aim is to seek the truth,

125. Cicero, *Academica*, I, xii.
126. Cicero, *De divinatione*, II, iii.
127. Lucretius, *De rerum natura*, III, 1048 and 1046.

knowledge, and certainty. The Epicureans, Stoics, and others thought they had found it. They established the sciences that we have and treated them as certain knowledge. Clytomachus, Carneades, and the Academicians despaired of their quest and considered that truth could not be conceived by the means at our disposal. Their conclusion is weakness and human ignorance; this school has the greatest following and the noblest adherents.

Pyrrho and other skeptics and epechists,[128] <<whose dogmas some ancients held to have been taken from Homer, the seven sages, Archilochus, Euripides, to whom they add Zeno, Democritus, Xenophanes,>> said that they were still searching for truth. They believe that those who think they have found truth are infinitely in error and that there is also too bold a vanity in the second degree, which asserts that human powers are not capable of attaining truth. For this claim to establish the measure of our power, to recognize and judge the difficulty of things, is a great and supreme knowledge of which they doubt that man is capable.

> *Whoever thinks he can know nothing does not know*
> *Whether he can know how it is that he can say that he knows*
>   *nothing.*[129]

The ignorance that knows itself, that judges itself and condemns itself, is not complete ignorance: to be so, it would have to be ignorant of itself. Thus the profession of the Pyrrhonists is to waver, doubt, and inquire, to be assured of nothing, to answer for nothing. Of the three activities of the soul—the imaginative, the appetitive and the consenting—they admit the first two; the last they consider and hold to be ambiguous, without inclination or approbation on one side or the other, however slight.

<<Zeno depicted with a gesture how he imagined the division of the faculties of the soul: the hand spread out and open was appearance, the hand half shut and the fingers bent a bit, consent; the closed fist, comprehension; when, with the left hand he proceeded to close that fist still tighter, knowledge.>>

Now this foundation of their judgment, straight and inflexible, receiving all objects without application or consent, leads them to their *ataraxia*, which is a condition of life that is peaceful, composed, exempt from the agitations we receive from the impression of opinion

---

128. Cf. Rabelais, *Tiers livre*, XXXVI, referring to those who suspend their judgment as "epechistes," from the Greek for "I hold back."

129. Lucretius, *De rerum natura*, IV, 470–1.

and knowledge that we think we have of things. From this arises fear, avarice, envy, immoderate desires, ambition, pride, superstition, the love of novelty, rebellion, disobedience, obstinacy, and the majority of bodily ills. In this way, to be sure, they exempt themselves from jealousy for their discipline, for they debate in a very mild manner. They do not fear rebuttal in their arguments. When they say that what is heavy sinks, they would be much annoyed if anyone believed them, and they seek to be contradicted so as to produce doubtfulness and suspension of judgment, which is their goal. They do not put forward their propositions, except to combat those they think we believe in. If you take their side, they will willingly take the contrary one to maintain: all is the same for them; they take no sides. If you assert that snow is black, they argue, on the contrary, that it is white. If you say that it is neither the one nor the other, it is up to them to maintain that it is both. If, judging with certainty, you hold that you know nothing about some matter, they will maintain that you do know it. Yes, and if in reference to a positive axiom, you assert that you are in doubt about it, they will proceed to argue that you do not doubt, and you cannot judge and establish that you are doubting. And by that extremity of doubt that unsettles itself, they separate themselves and cut themselves off from numerous opinions, even of those who, in various fashions, have maintained doubt and ignorance.

<Why are they not allowed to doubt, they say, as among the dogmatists it is allowed for one to say green, the other yellow—is there anything you can propose to advocate and deny that it is not possible to consider ambiguous? And, why not, when others are led—either by the custom of their country, or by the way their parents brought them up, or by chance, as if by storm, without judgment or choice, indeed, most often before the age of discretion—to such and such an opinion, either to the Stoic or the Epicurean sect, to which they find themselves apprenticed, enslaved, and bound as if it were something they had bitten into and could not let go. *"They cling to any discipline as to a rock, as if a storm had blown them there."*[130]>> Why should it not also be granted to them to maintain their liberty and to consider things without obligation and servitude? <<*"Truer and more independent, in that they have the complete power of judging."*[131] Is it not some advantage to find oneself freed of the necessity that binds others?>> Is it not worth more to remain in suspense than to tangle oneself in so many errors produced

130. Cicero, *Academica*, II, iii.
131. Cicero, *Academica*, II, iii.

by human imagination? Is it not worth more to suspend one's conviction than to get mixed up in these seditious and quarrelsome divisions?
<<What shall I choose?—Whatever you like, as long as you choose!—
There's a stupid reply, which it seems is what every dogmatism comes
to, by which we are not allowed not to know what we do not know.>>
Take the most famous position; it will never be so certain that to defend
it you will not need to attack and combat hundreds of opposing positions. Is it not better to stay out of that scuffle? You are permitted to
espouse, as if it were your honor and your life, Aristotle's belief on the
eternity of the soul and to deny and rebut Plato on this point; and are
they forbidden to doubt this? <<If it is permissible for Panaetius to suspend his judgment about auspices, dreams, oracles, prophecies, on
which matters the Stoics have no doubt, why will not a sage dare in all
things what this one here dares in matters that he has learned from his
masters' establishment by common consent of the school to which he
belongs and whose beliefs he professes?>> If it is a child who is making
a judgment, he does not know what is the case; if it is a learned man, he
is prejudiced. They have reserved for themselves a wonderful advantage
in combat, having no need to protect themselves. It does not matter
that they are attacked, provided that they attack, and they make their
work of everything. If they conquer, your proposition is defective; if you
win, theirs is. If they fail, they verify ignorance; if you fail, you verify it.
If they prove that nothing is known, well and good; if they don't know
how to prove it, that's good too.> <<"If equal arguments are found for and
against on the same subject, judgment will be suspended more easily on
either side."[132]

And they make much more of finding easily why something is false
than they do of finding it is true; and of what is not, than what is; and of
what they do not believe, than what they do believe.>>

Their manners of speaking are: I establish nothing; it is no more
thus than thus or than neither one nor the other; I do not in the least
understand; the appearances are equal everywhere; the right to speak
for and against is equal. <<Nothing seems true that cannot seem false.>>
Their sacramental word is *epecho*; that is to say, I hold back, I do not
budge. These are their refrains and others of similar substance. Their
effect is a pure, complete, and entirely perfect suspension of judgment.
They use their reason to inquire and to debate, but not to stop and
choose. Anyone who imagines a perpetual confession of ignorance, a
judgment without bent or inclination, on any occasion whatsoever, will

132. Cicero, *Academica*, II, xii.

understand Pyrrhonism. I am expressing their fantasy as well as I can, since many find it difficult to grasp, and the authors themselves represent it a bit obscurely and in different ways.

As to the actions of life, they follow the common fashion: they lend and accommodate themselves to the impulsions and constraints of the passions, to the constitutions of laws and customs, and to the tradition of the arts. <<"For God did not want us to know these things but only to make use of them.">>[133] Here they let their common actions guide them to these things without any opinions or judgment. This is why I cannot square this presentation to what is said about Pyrrho. They portray him as stupid and immobile, following a wild and unsociable course of life, waiting for carts to hit him, risking his life at precipices, refusing to conform to the laws. This goes beyond his discipline. He did not want to make himself a stone or a stump. He wanted to make himself a living, discoursing, thinking man, depending on and making use of all those bodily and spiritual parts in the prescribed and proper way. The fantastic, imaginary, and false privileges of governing, ordering, and establishing truth that man has usurped, he has renounced and abandoned in good faith.

<<Indeed, there is no sect that is not constrained to allow its wise man to go along with a number of things neither understood, nor perceived, nor assented to, if he wants to live. And when he goes to sea he follows this plan, not knowing if this will be useful to him, and he relies on the ship's being good, the pilot experienced, the weather appropriate—all merely probable circumstances. He is bound to act according to this and to allow himself to behave in conformity with appearances, provided they offer nothing expressly to the contrary. He has a body; he has a soul. His senses impel him; his mind agitates him. Even though he does not find in himself that peculiar and singular mark of making a judgment and though he sees that he must not give his consent, since something false may look like the truth, he does not stop conducting the affairs of his life fully and conveniently. How many arts are there that profess to consist of conjecture rather than of knowledge, that do not decide on true and false and follow only what appears? There are, they say, both true and false, and there is in us something to search for it, but not something with which to attain it as with a touchstone. We do much better if we let ourselves feel our way without inquiring into the order of the world. A soul armed against prejudice has a wonderful advance on tranquillity. People who judge

133. Cicero, De divinatione, I, xviii.

and control their judges never submit as they should. But to religious and political laws, how much more docile and easy to lead are simple and incurious minds than those minds that survey and instruct on divine and human causes!>>

No human invention has so much verisimilitude and utility. It presents man naked and empty, recognizing his natural weakness, fit to receive some outside power from on high, stripped of human knowledge, and so much more likely to receive in himself divine knowledge, <annihilating his judgment to make more room for faith,> <<neither disbelieving>> nor establishing any dogma <against common observances; humble, obedient, teachable, studious; sworn enemy of heresy> and thus exempting himself from the vain and irreligious opinions introduced by false sects. <He is a blank tablet prepared to take from God's finger such forms as it pleases him to write on it. The more we turn back and commit ourselves to God and renounce ourselves, the more we are worth.> Receive in good part, says Ecclesiastes, things as they are presented to your sight and your taste, from day to day; other things are beyond your knowledge.[134] <<"*The Lord knows the thoughts of man and knows they are vain.*"[135]

That is how, of the three general schools of philosophy, two profess doubt and ignorance, and in that of the dogmatists, which is the third, it is easy to discover that the majority have taken on the appearance of self-confidence only so as to look better. They have not thought so much of establishing some certainty for us as of showing how far they have gone in the quest for truth, <<"*which the learned pretend to more than they know.*">>[136] Timaeus, having to instruct Socrates about what he knew of the gods, the world, and men, proposes to talk as one man to another, and that is sufficient if his arguments are as probable as the next man's. For exact arguments are not in his grasp, nor in any mortal grasp. That is what one of his followers copied in this way: "*I will explain as far as I can; yet not as if I were Pythias Apollo, saying things that are fixed and certain, but rather like a mere man, following probable conjectures.*"[137] And this was on the subject of the contempt of death, a natural and popular topic. Elsewhere he translated the very statement of Plato: "*If it happens that, speaking of the nature of the gods and of the origin of the world, I cannot reach the goal that I set myself, you must not*

134. This seems to be a paraphrase of Ecclesiastes 3:22.
135. Psalms 94:11.
136. Livy, *Histories*, XXVI, xxii
137. Cicero, *Tusculan Disputations*, I, ix.

be surprised; for you must remember that I who speak and you who judge are only men, and if I give you probabilities, do not look for more.">>[138]

Aristotle usually heaps up on us a great number of other opinions and other beliefs in order to compare his and to make us see how much further he has gone and how much more closely he has approached verisimilitude, for truth is not judged by the authority and witness of another. <<However, Epicurus religiously avoided citing others in his writings.>> Aristotle is the prince of dogmatists, and yet we learn from him that knowing much is the occasion for doubting more. We often see him deliberately covering himself with obscurity so thick and inextricable that we can make nothing of his opinion. This is, in fact, a Pyrrhonism under an affirmative form.

<<Hear the protestation of Cicero, who explains the idea of others by his own: *"Those who investigate what we think on every subject act with more curiosity than is necessary. This principle in philosophy of discussing everything without deciding anything, produced by Socrates, repeated by Arcesilaus, confirmed by Carneades, is still vigorous in our day. We are of the school that says the false is everywhere mixed with the true and is so like it that no criterion allows us to judge and to decide with certainty.">>*[139]

<Why have not only Aristotle, but most philosophers, affected difficulty, if not to stress the vanity of the subject and to divert the curiosity of our minds, giving it somewhere to feed in gnawing at this hollow and fleshless bone? <<Clitomachus asserted that he had never been able to understand from the writings of Carneades what his opinion was.>> That is why Epicurus avoided perspicuity with his own people and why Heraclitus was called *skoteinos*, the dark. Difficulty is a coin <<that the learned use, like people who do conjuring tricks, in order not to reveal the vanity of their art,>> and which human stupidity easily accepts as payment:

> *Among the empty headed, he is more famous because of his*
> *   obscure tongue.*
> *For the stolid admire and love more*
> *The hidden things that lurk under twisted words.>*[140]

<<Cicero reproaches some of his friends for being accustomed to give more time to astrology, law, dialectic, and geometry than these arts

138. Plato, *Timaeus* (trans. Cicero), chapter 3.
139. Cicero, *De natura deorum*, I, v.
140. Lucretius, *De rerum natura*, I, 640–2.

deserve; this diverted them from the more useful and honorable duties
of life. The Cyrenaic philosophers despised equally physics and dialec-
tic. Zeno, at the very beginning of the books of his *Republic*, declared
useless all the liberal arts.>>

Chrysippus said that what Plato and Aristotle wrote on logic must
have been written as a game and for practice, and he could not believe
they had said anything serious on so frivolous a subject. <<Plutarch said
the same about metaphysics.>> Epicurus would have said it also about
rhetoric, grammar, <<poetry, mathematics, and, except for physics,
about all the sciences.>> And Socrates, too, about everything except for
what deals with behavior and life. <<Whatever he was asked about, he
always led the inquirer to give an account of the present and past conditions of his life, which he examined and assessed, considering any other
training inferior and superfluous.

*"That literature which has been of no benefit to virtue in those who are
learned in it gives me little pleasure."*>>[141] Most of the arts themselves
have been mistrusted in this way by learning. But men did not think it
unsuitable to exercise and entertain their minds with things that did not
have any profitable solidity.

Moreover, some have considered Plato a dogmatist; others, a doubter;
others, in certain things, the former; and in other things, the latter.

<<The leader of Plato's dialogues, Socrates, always goes on inquiring
and stirring up dispute—never closing it, never bringing it to a satisfac-
tory conclusion—and says that he has no knowledge except for knowing how to make objections. Homer, as their author, laid the
foundations equally for all the schools of philosophy in order to show
how little he cared which way we might go. It is said that the different
schools originated from Plato. Indeed, in my opinion, never was
instruction wavering and assertive of nothing if his was not. Socrates
used to say that wise women,[142] in taking up their profession of making
others give birth, abandon the profession of giving birth themselves,
and that he, in virtue of the title of wise man the gods had conferred on
him, had also rid himself, in his physical and mental love, of the power
of giving birth; he was satisfied with helping and favoring with his assistance those who were in labor, opening their organs, greasing their pas-
sageways, facilitating the issue of their offspring, evaluating it, baptizing
it, nourishing it, strengthening it—bringing his skill to bear on the dangers and successes of others.>>

141. Sallust, as paraphrased by Justus Lipsius, *Politicorum*, I, 10.
142. That is, midwives.

It is the same with authors of the third type: <as the ancients have remarked on the writings of Anaxagoras, Democritus, Parmenides, Xenophanes, and others,> they have a form of writing that is doubtful in substance and a plan that is investigative rather than instructive, while they sprinkle their style with dogmatic accents. Is that not equally evident <<both in Seneca and>> in Plutarch? <<How much they say, now with one face, now with another, for those who look at them closely! And those who reconcile legal experts with one another should first reconcile each one with himself.

Plato seems to me to have loved this form of philosophizing through dialogues, and to have used it deliberately, in order to put the diversity and varieties of his own ideas more respectably in diverse mouths.

To treat matters in different ways is as good as to treat them uniformly and better, that is, more fully and more usefully. Let us take an example from our society: legal judgments constitute the extreme point of dogmatic and resolute speaking; yet the most exemplary ones that our courts present to the people as fit to nourish in them the reverence that is owed to the dignity of those bodies, chiefly because of the competence of the agents, acquire their beauty not from the conclusion, which is familiar to them and which is common to every judge, so much as from the dispute, the excitement of diversified and contrary arguments to which the matter of law is subject.

And the widest field for the reprehensions of philosophers against one another arises from the contradictions and differences in which each of them finds himself entangled, either on purpose, in order to exhibit the vacillation of the human mind on all subjects, or unintentionally, compelled by the glibness and incomprehensibility of every subject matter.>>

What is the meaning of this refrain: in a slippery and shifting place, let us suspend our judgment? For, as Euripides says,

> The works of God
> Cross us in various ways,[143]

<which is like what Empedocles often scattered in his books, as if moved by a divine rage and compelled by truth. No, no, we feel nothing, we see nothing; all things are obscure to us, there is nothing of which we can establish that it is;> <<remember that divine word: *"The thoughts of mortal men are timorous, and our contrivances and*

---

143. Plutarch, *Des oracles qui ont cessé* (trans. Amyot), 35.

precautions uncertain.">>[144] We should not find it strange if hunters despairing of their prey have not stopped enjoying the chase, since study is in itself a pleasant occupation, so pleasant that, among pleasurable sensations, the Stoics forbid that one, too, which comes from the exercise of the mind; they want to rein it in <<and find it intemperate to know too much.>>

Democritus, when he had eaten at his table figs that tasted of honey, suddenly began to search in his mind for the source of that unaccustomed sweetness and, to enlighten himself, was going to get up from the table to look at the place from which those figs had been gathered; his maidservant, who had heard the cause of his excitement, said to him, laughing, that he should not trouble himself any more about that, since she had put them in a container that had held honey. He was annoyed because she had removed the occasion for his investigation and had robbed him of a subject for curiosity. "Go along," he said, "you have displeased me; still, I will not give up seeking the cause as if it were natural." <<And he willingly went on to find some true reason for a false and supposed effect.>> This story about a famous and great philosopher shows us clearly the passion for study that amuses us in the pursuit of things of whose acquisition we have no hope. Plutarch narrates a similar case of someone who did not want to be enlightened about something of which he was in doubt so as not to lose the pleasure of searching for it, like the other person who did not want his physician to remove the thirst of his fever, so that he would not lose the pleasure of assuaging it by having something to drink. *"It is better to learn useless things than to learn nothing."*[145]

In the same way, in any food there is often nothing but pleasure; not everything pleasant we take in is nutritious or healthful. Similarly, what our minds take in of knowledge does not stop being enjoyable even though it is neither nourishing nor salutary.>>

<Here is what they say: The consideration of nature is fitting food for our minds; it lifts us up and swells us out, makes us despise low and earthly things in comparison with those that are superior and celestial. The investigation itself of obscure and great things is very pleasant, even for one who acquires only reverence for them and the fear of making a judgment on them. These are the words of their profession. The vain image of that accursed curiosity is to be seen still more explicitly in that

---

144. Wisdom of Solomon 9:14: "For the reasoning of mortals is worthless, and our designs are likely to fail."

145. Seneca, *Epistles*, LXXXVIII.

other example that they so often quote as an honor. Eudoxus hoped and prayed to the gods that he might once see the sun from close by and understand its form, its magnitude, and its beauty even if he would be at once burned up by it. He wishes, at the cost of his life, to acquire one item of knowledge of whose use and possession he will at the same time be deprived, and for this sudden and fleeting knowledge, to lose all other knowledge that he has and that he might afterward acquire.>

I am not easily convinced that Epicurus, Plato, and Pythagoras have given us their atoms, their ideas, and their numbers as real money. They were too wise to establish their articles of faith on the basis of things so uncertain and so debatable. But into this obscurity and ignorance of the world, each of these great persons labored to bring some sort of semblance of light, and they occupied their minds with inventions that had at least a pleasant and subtle appearance <<provided that, however false, it could be maintained against arguments to the contrary. *"These things are invented by the ingenuity of each, not by the power of knowledge."*>>[146] One of the ancients, who was reproached for professing philosophy of which, however, in his own judgment he did not take great stock, replied that this was really to philosophize. They wanted to consider everything, balance everything, and they found that occupation fitting for the natural curiosity in us. Some things they wrote to meet the need of the general public, like their religions, and with that consideration it was reasonable that they did not wait to strip common opinions to the skin in order not to make trouble for obedience to the laws and customs of their country.

<<Plato treats this mystery with an obvious enough game. For when he writes in his own name, he prescribes nothing for certain. When he acts as legislator, he adopts a dictatorial and assertive style and yet boldly mixes in the most fantastic of his inventions, as useful in persuading the common people as they are ridiculous in persuading himself, knowing how apt we are to receive all impressions and, above all, the wildest and most outrageous.

And therefore in his *Laws* he takes great care that only verses whose fabulous fictions tend toward some useful end are sung in public, and since it is so easy to imprint all sorts of phantasms on the human mind, he thinks it wrong not to feed it with profitable lies rather than with lies that are useless or harmful. He says quite bluntly in his *Republic* that for the good of men it is often necessary to dupe them. It is easy to distinguish, on the one hand, sects that have preferred to follow truth, on the

146. Seneca, *Suasoriae*, IV.

other, utility, by which the latter have gained credit. It is the misery of our condition that often what presents itself to our imagination as truest does not present itself as the most useful for our lives. The boldest schools—Epicurean, Pyrrhonist, New Academy—are still constrained, in the last analysis, to conform to civil law.>>

There are other subjects philosophers have tossed about, some to the left, some to the right, each laboring to give it some countenance, whether it deserves it or not. For, having found nothing so abstruse that they would not venture to speak of it, they were often forced to invent feeble and foolish conjectures, not that they themselves took them as a foundation, or to establish some truth, but only for the exercise of their ingenuity: <<"Not so much that they believed what they said, as that they seemed to want to exercise their minds by the difficulty of the subject matter.">>[147]

And if we did not understand it in this way, how would we account for such great inconstancy, variety, and vanity of opinions as we see have been produced by those excellent and admirable souls? For, to take an example, what is more vain than to want to guess at God by our analogies and conjectures, to regulate him and the world according to our capacity and our laws, and to make use at the expense of divinity of that small sample of sufficiency it has pleased him to dispense to our natural condition? And because we cannot extend our vision as far as his glorious throne, are we to bring it down here to our corruption and to our wretchedness?

Of all the human and ancient opinions concerning religion, the one that has the most likelihood and most excuse, it seems to me, is the one that acknowledges God as an incomprehensible power, origin and conservator of all things, all goodness, all perfection, receiving and taking in good part the honor and reverence that human beings render him under some aspect, under any name or manner whatever:

> <<Jupiter, ruler over all things,
> Father and mother of kings and gods.[148]

This zeal has always been looked upon favorably by heaven. All policies have borne the fruit of their devotion: men and impious actions have been distinguished by their results. The pagan histories recognize dignity, order, justice, as well as prodigies and oracles used for profit and instruction in their fabulous religions, God, in his mercy, deigning

147. Quintilian, *Institutio oratoria*, II, 17, 4.
148. Soranus, quoted by Saint Augustine, *City of God*, IX, ii.

to encourage at random by these temporal advantages the tender principles of such rough knowledge of him as natural reason has given us through the false images of our dreams.

Those that man has forged by his own invention are not only false but injurious as well.>>

And of all the religions that Saint Paul found accredited at Athens, the one dedicated to a hidden and unknown divinity seemed to him the most excusable.[149]

<<Pythagoras came closest to the truth, holding that the knowledge of this first cause and being of beings must be indefinite, without prescription, without declaration; that it was nothing but the extreme effort of our imagination toward perfection, each one amplifying the idea according to his capacity. But if Numa undertook to adjust the devotion of his people to this project, to attach them to a purely mental religion without preset object and without material admixture, he was undertaking something of no use—the human mind would not know how to maintain itself floating in that infinity of unformed thoughts; it needs to compile a certain image for its model. Thus divine majesty has in some way or other allowed itself to be circumscribed in corporeal limits: its supernatural and celestial sacraments are signs of our terrestrial condition; its adoration is expressed by sensible offices and words, for it is man who believes and who prays. I leave aside the other arguments that are employed on this subject. But it would be difficult to make me believe that the sight of our crucifixes and the painting of that cruel agony, that the ornaments and ceremonious movements of our churches, that the voices adapted to the devotion of our thought and that stirring of the senses do not heat up the souls of the peoples with a religious passion that has a very useful effect.>>[150]

In the religions we have produced, as necessity required, within that universal blindness, I have been, it seems to me, most willingly attached to those who adore the sun,

> . . . the common light,
> The eye of the world; and if God above all has eyes,
> The sun's rays are his radiant eyes,
> Give life to all, maintain and protect us,
> And watch the deeds of men in this world:
> This fair, this great sun who gives us the seasons,

149. Acts 17:23.
150. Plutarch, *Lives*, XLI, "Life of Numa" (trans. Amyot).

According to how it enters and leaves its twelve houses;
Who fills the universe with his acknowledged powers,
Who dissipates the clouds with a glance of his eye:
The mind, the soul of the world, ardent and flamboyant,
Turning the whole heaven in the course of a day;
Full of immense greatness, round, moving, and steady;
Who holds below him the whole world as his limit;
At rest without rest; idle and never resting;
Eldest son of nature and father of the day.[151]

In addition to its magnitude and beauty, it is the part of the machine we discover at the greatest distance from us and, for that reason, so little known that it was forgivable that they entered into admiration and reverence for it.

<<Thales, who was the first to inquire into such matters, thought God was a spirit who made all things of water; Anaximander, that the gods lived and died at different seasons and that there were worlds infinite in number; Anaximenes, that the air was God, who was created and immense, always moving. Anaxagoras was the first who held the description and mode of being of all things to be governed by the force and reason of an infinite mind. Alcmaeon gave divinity to the sun, the moon, the stars, and the soul. Pythagoras made God a spirit spread by nature through all things, from which our souls are extracted; Parmenides, a circle surrounding the heavens, and preserving the world by the brilliance of its light. Empedocles said that the four natures of which all things are made were gods. Protagoras said that he did not have to say whether they existed or not or what they were. Democritus sometimes asserted that images and their circular motions are gods, sometimes that the nature emitting those images are gods, and then [that] our knowledge and intelligence [are gods]. Plato distributes his belief under several aspects: he says in the *Timaeus* that the father of the world cannot be named; in the *Laws*, that we must not inquire into his being; and elsewhere in those same books he makes the world, the heavens, the stars, the earth, and our souls into gods and accepts as well those who are received by ancient tradition in each republic. Xenophon reports a similar problem in Socrates' teaching: sometimes he declines to inquire into the form of God, and then he has him establish that the sun is God and the soul, God; that there is only one, and then that there are a number. Speusippus, Plato's nephew, makes God a certain force that governs things and is animate. Aristotle sometimes says it

151. Ronsard, *Remontrance au peuple de France*.

is mind, sometimes the world; sometimes he gives this world another master, and sometimes he makes God the heat of the heavens. Xenocrates has eight gods: the five named for the planets, the sixth composed of all the fixed stars as of its members, the seventh and eighth of the sun and moon. Heraclides Ponticus just wanders from one opinion to another, and finally deprives God of sentience and makes him move from one form to another, and then says he is the heavens and the earth. Theophrastus strolls with the same irresolution among all his fantasies, attributing the management of the world now to intelligence, now to the heavens, now to the stars. Strato says that it is nature that has the force of engendering, increasing, and decreasing, without form or feeling; Zeno, that it is natural law, commanding good and prohibiting evil, a law that animates and removes the usual gods—Jupiter, Juno, Vesta; Diogenes Apolloniates, that it is air.[152] Xenophanes makes God spherical, seeing, hearing, not breathing, having nothing in common with human nature. Ariston considers the form of God incomprehensible, deprives him of sense and does not know whether he is animate or something else; Cleanthes makes him sometimes reason, sometimes the world, sometimes the soul of nature, sometimes the supreme heat surrounding and enveloping everything. Perseus, who was Zeno's student, held that those have been called God who had contributed some notable benefit to human life, and even the profitable things themselves. Chrysippus made a confused muddle of all the preceding sentiments and counted also, among the thousand forms of God he created, the men who are immortalized. Diagoras and Theodorus quite dryly deny that there are gods. Epicurus makes the gods glowing, transparent, and permeable, located between two worlds, as if between two strongholds, safe from blows, provided with a human shape and with our members, which are of no use to them.

> *I have always said and will always say that there are gods,*
> *But I do believe they do not care what humankind does.*[153]

Have confidence in your philosophy; boast of having found the bean in the cake when you observe the racket made by so many philosophical brains! The confusion of forms in the world has meant that when I compare them, the different customs and fantasies other than mine do not so much displease as instruct me; they do not so much make me proud as humiliate me; and every choice but that which comes

152. Reading "air" for *aage*.
153. Ennius, cited by Cicero, *De divinatione*, II, i.

expressly from the hand of God seems to me of little weight. I leave aside monstrous and unnatural modes of life. The customs of the world are no less contrary to one another on this subject than are the schools, by which we may learn that fortune itself is no less diverse and variable than our reason, nor more blind and unconsidered.>>

The things we know least are most appropriate for deification. How to make gods of ourselves, as the ancients did—that surpasses the limits of folly in discourse. I would rather have followed those who adored the serpent, the dog, and the ox, insofar as their nature and their being are less well-known, and we have a better right to imagine whatever we like of those beasts and to attribute to them extraordinary powers. But to have made gods of our condition, of whose imperfection we ought to be aware, to have attributed to those gods desire, anger, vengeance, marriages, generations and family relations, love and jealousy, our organs and our bones, our fevers and our pleasures, <<our deaths, our sepulchers>>—that must have issued from a marvelous intoxication of human understanding,

> <Those things standing so far from divinity,
> Which are unworthy to be counted in the number of the
> gods.>[154]

<<"Their forms, ages, clothing, genealogy, marriages, alliances, all are represented on the model of human weakness; for they are subjected to the same troubles. We speak of the passions of the gods, of their disappointments or their rages.">>[155] It is as if we had attributed divinity <<not only to faith, to virtue, to honor, concord, liberty, victory, piety, but also to lust, fraud, death, envy, old age, misery,>> to fear, fever, and misfortune, and other injuries of our frail and decrepit life.

> <What use is it to introduce our mores in the temples?
> Oh, souls bent to earth and denuded of the heavens!>[156]

<<The Egyptians, with an impudent prudence, forbade anyone, on pain of hanging, to say that Serapis and Isis, their gods, had once been men, and no one was ignorant of the fact that they had been so. And Varro says that their effigy, represented with its finger on the mouth, signified this mysterious command to their priests—to be silent about

154. Lucretius, *De rerum natura*, V, 123–4.
155. Cicero, *De natura deorum*, I, xxviii.
156. Persius, *Satires*, II, 61–2.

their mortal origin—as a reason that would necessarily cancel all veneration of them.>>

Since man wanted so much to match himself with God, he would have done better, says Cicero, to take to himself the conditions of divinity and to bring those conditions down here rather than to send up there his corruption and his wretchedness; but to tell the truth, he did both in a number of ways, with equal folly in forming his opinions.

When the philosophers spell out the hierarchy of their gods and make them eager to distinguish their alliances, their charges, and their power, I cannot believe that they are speaking with certainty. When Plato describes Pluto's orchard for us, and the bodily comforts and pains that yet await us after the ruin and annihilation of our bodies, and accommodates them to the feelings we have in this life—

> Secret paths hide, and a myrtle grove covers them;
> Their cares do not leave them even in death.[157]

—when Mohammed promises his people a carpeted paradise paved with gold and jewels, peopled with girls of great beauty, with wines and rare food, I see clearly that they are mockers who are catering to our stupidity to sweeten and attract us by these opinions and hopes, suited to our mortal appetite. <<Even some of our own people have fallen into a like error, promising themselves, after the resurrection, an earthly and temporal life accompanied by all sorts of pleasures and worldly comforts.>> Do we believe that Plato—he who had such lofty ideas and so great an acquaintance with divinity that the surname divine has remained with him—thought man, this poor creature, had in him anything applicable to that incomprehensible power? Or that he believed our languishing grasp was able, or the force of our sense robust enough, to participate in eternal blessedness or pain? We would have to say to him on behalf of human reason:

"If the pleasures you promise us in the other life are those I have felt down here, that has nothing in common with infinity. If all my five senses were naturally the height of gaiety and my soul filled with all the contentment it could desire and hope for, we know what that would be: it would still be nothing. If there is anything that is mine, there is nothing divine in it. If it is nothing but what can belong to our present condition, it cannot be of any value. <<All the contentment of mortals is mortal.>> The recognition of our kinsfolk, of our children and our friends, if it can touch and tickle us in the other world, if we still cling

157. Virgil, *Aeneid*, VI, 443–4.

to such a pleasure, we are among earthly and finite comforts. We cannot fittingly conceive of the grandeur of those high and divine promises, if we can conceive them at all; to imagine them fittingly, we must imagine them as unimaginable, inexpressible, and incomprehensible, <<and wholly other than those of our miserable experience.>> 'The eye cannot see,' says Saint Paul, 'the good fortune God has prepared for his own, nor can it mount into the heart of man.'[158] And if, to make us capable of this, our being is reformed and remade (as you say, Plato, by your purifications), such a change must be so extreme and so universal that by physical teaching this will no longer be ourselves:

> <It was Hector, then, who fought in battle, and he
> Who was drawn by the Thracian horse was not Hector.>[159]

"It will be something else that will receive those recompenses,

> <. . . what is changed dissolves; therefore it perishes,
> For the parts cross over and change in order.>[160]

"For, in the metempsychosis of Pythagoras and the change of habitation that he imagines for souls, do we think that the lion in which Caesar's soul resides embraces the passions that touched Caesar, <<or that it is he? If it were once more Caesar, they would be right who, combating that opinion against Plato, objected to him that the son would be able to straddle his mother, clothed with the body of a mule, and similar absurdities. And do we think>> that, in the changes occurring to the bodies of animals in others of the same species, the newcomers are not different from their predecessors? They say that the ashes of the phoenix engender a worm and then another phoenix; as to that second phoenix, who can imagine that it is not different from the first? Take the worms that make our silk: we see them die, as it were, and dry up, and from this same body is produced a butterfly, and from it another worm, which it would be absurd to think was again the first one. What has once ceased to be is no longer:

> If time collected together our matter
> After death, and restored the order that it now has,
> And if the lights of life were again given us,

158. 1 Corinthians 2:9.
159. Ovid, *Tristia*, III, ii, 27–8.
160. Lucretius, *De rerum natura*, III, 376–7.

Still what was done again would not pertain to us at all,
Once our memories were interrupted.[161]

"And Plato, when you say elsewhere that it will be the spiritual part of
man to which it will belong to enjoy the recompenses of the other life,
you tell us something just as unlikely:

<It is evident that, torn from its roots,
The eye itself would see nothing, separated from the whole
    body.>[162]

"For, as far as that goes, it will no longer be man, nor consequently ourselves, to whom this enjoyment will belong; for we are built of two principal, essential parts, whose separation is death and the ruin of our
being,

<For the cessation of life is cast forth, and
All motions stray distractedly everywhere away from the
    senses.>[163]

"We do not say that man is suffering when the worms eat the organs
from which he lives and when the earth consumes him,

And this is nothing to us, who consist of
The closely joined union and conjunction of body and
    soul."[164]

Moreover, on what foundation of their justice can the gods recognize and recompense man for his good and virtuous actions after his
death when it is they themselves who have guided and produced those
actions in him? And why do they take offense and punish him for his
vicious actions when they themselves have produced him in that faulty
condition and when, with a single inclination of their will, they can
keep him from erring? And would Epicurus make this objection to
Plato with every appearance of human rationality <<if he did not often
protect himself with this statement: that it is impossible for mortal
nature to establish anything with certainty about the immortal?>> Our

161. Lucretius, *De rerum natura*, III, 847–51.
162. Lucretius, *De rerum natura*, III, 561–2.
163. Lucretius, *De rerum natura*, III, 872–3.
164. Lucretius, *De rerum natura*, III, 857–8.

nature only leads us astray everywhere, but especially when it meddles in divine matters. Who feels this more clearly than we do? For although we have given it certain and infallible principles, although we light its footsteps by the sacred lamp of the truth that it has pleased God to communicate to us, nevertheless, however little it deviates from the ordinary path and turns away and moves aside from the way traced and beaten by the Church, we see daily how entirely it at once destroys, hampers, and hobbles itself, turning and floating on that vast, troubled and billowing sea of human opinions, without bridle and without end. As soon as it loses that great common path, it goes dividing and dissipating itself on a thousand different routes.

Man can be nothing but what he is, nor imagine except according to his capacity. <It is a greater presumption, says Plutarch, for those who are only men to undertake to speak and reason about gods and demigods than it is for a man ignorant of music to presume to judge those who are singing, or for a man who has never been in battle to dispute about arms and war, presuming to understand by some frivolous guesswork the details of an art beyond his knowledge.> The ancients thought, so I believe, that they could do something for divine greatness by likening it to man, clothing it with his faculties, investing it with his good moods <<and more shameful necessities,>> offering it our food to eat, <<our dances, mummeries, and farces to enjoy,>> our clothes to cover it and our houses to live in, caressing it with the scent of incense and the sounds of music, with festoons and bouquets, <<and, to accommodate it to our vicious passions, flattering its justice with an inhuman vengeance, pleasing it with the ruin and dissipation of things created and conserved by it (like Tiberius Sempronius, who, as a sacrifice to Vulcan, had burned the rich spoils and arms he had gained from his enemies in Sardinia; and Paul Emilius, to Mars and to Minerva, those of Macedonia; and Alexander, who, when he arrived at the Indian Ocean, as a tribute to Thetis, threw into the sea several large gold vases); and besides, filling their altars with a slaughter, not only of innocent beasts, but also of men,>> in a way that a number of nations, and ours among others, made an ordinary custom. And I believe there are none that have failed to try this,

<. . . four young
Sons of Sulmo, as many produced by Ufens,
He snatched living and immolated them to the infernal
shades.>[165]

165. Virgil, Aeneid, X, 507–9.

<<The Getae consider themselves immortal; for them death is nothing but moving toward their god Zamolxis. Every five years they dispatch one among them in his direction in order to ask for things that are necessary. This deputy is chosen by lot. And the manner of dispatching him, after he has been told of his task, is that, of those who are present, three hold up as many javelins at which the others throw him with the force of their arms. If he happens to be run through at a mortal place and if this happens suddenly, that is certain evidence for them of divine favor; if he escapes, they consider him evil and execrable and assign someone else to the same fate.

Amestris, the mother of Xerxes, when she was old, had at one time buried alive four striplings from the best houses of Persia, following the religion of the country, in order to gratify some subterranean god.

Even today the idols of Themistitan are cemented with the blood of infants and love the sacrifice of only those childish, pure souls—justice hungry for the blood of innocents:

So many evils can religion recommend.>>[166]

<The Carthaginians sacrificed their own children to Saturn, and those who had none bought some, while the father and mother were nevertheless forced to be present at that ceremony with a cheerful and contented countenance.> It was a strange idea to wish to requite divine goodness with our affliction, like the Lacedaemonians, who courted their Diana by torturing young boys whom they had whipped for her sake, often mortally. It was a barbarous humor to want to gratify the architect by overturning his building and to wish to assure the pain due to the guilty by the punishment of the nonguilty, and that at the port of Aulis poor Iphigenia, by her death and immolation cleared before God the army of the Greeks of the offenses they had committed—

<A virgin, impurely, at the very time of her betrothal,
She fell, sadly, victim of her father's slaying>[167]

—<<and those two fair and generous souls of the two Deciuses, father and son, to propitiate the favor of the gods for Roman affairs, let themselves be thrown headlong into the thick of their enemies.

"How great was the iniquity of the gods, that they could not be favorable

166. Lucretius, *De rerum natura*, I, 102.
167. Lucretius, *De rerum natura*, I, 99–100.

to the Roman people unless such men died?">>[168] Besides, it is not for the criminal to have himself whipped according to his assessment and when he likes; it is for the judge, <who counts as punishment only the suffering he orders <<and cannot attribute to punishment what comes with the sufferer's consent. Divine vengeance presupposes complete dissent from his justice and our pain.>>

And the whim of Policrates, tyrant of Samos, was ridiculous; to interrupt the course of his continual happiness and to compensate for it, he had thrown into the sea the most costly and most precious jewel that he owned, thinking that through this deliberate evil he would satisfy the revolution and vicissitude of fortune,> <<and fortune, to laugh at his ineptitude, had that same jewel once more returned to his hands in the belly of a fish.>> And then <<what use are the rendings and dismemberings of the Corybants, the Maenads, and in our day, the Mohammedans, who slash their faces, stomachs, limbs, to gratify their prophet, given that>> the offense consists in the will, not <<in the breast, eyes, genitals, roundness,>> shoulders, and windpipe. <<*"So great is the fury of a mind disturbed and unhinged, as if the gods could be appeased by cruelties surpassing those of men."*[169]

This natural structure concerns in its application not only ourselves but also the service of God and of other men: it is an injustice to distort it deliberately, as it is to kill ourselves for any reason whatsoever. It seems great cowardice and treason to abuse and corrupt the functions of the body, stupid and in bondage, in order to spare the soul the trouble of guiding them according to reason.

"What is it they fear will irritate the gods, they who believe they can propitiate them in this way? Men have been castrated to serve the pleasure of kings, but no slave has ever castrated himself when his master ordered him no longer to be a man.">>[170]

Thus they filled their religion with many bad results:

> . . . it was often
> *Religion that produced criminal and impious effects.*[171]

But nothing of ours can be furnished or attributed to the divine nature that does not stain and mark it with some imperfection. That

168. Cicero, *De natura deorum*, III, 6.
169. Saint Augustine, *City of God*, VI, x.
170. Saint Augustine, *City of God*, VI, x.
171. Lucretius, *De rerum natura*, I, 83–4.

infinite beauty, power, and goodness—how little can it admit any correspondence and similarity to something as abject as we are without badly
damaging and diminishing its divine greatness?

<<*"God's weakness is stronger than men, and God's stupidity is wiser
than men."*[172]

Stilpon the philosopher, when asked if the gods rejoiced in our honors and sacrifices, replied: "You are indiscreet; let us withdraw if you
want to talk about that.">>[173]

Yet we prescribe limits for him; we besiege his power with our arguments (I call arguments our reveries and our dreams, with the exception of philosophy, which speaks pure nonsense and wickedness driven
mad by argument, but argument of a particular form); we want to
enslave God to the vain and feeble appearances of our understanding,
him who has made both us and our knowledge. Since nothing comes
of nothing, God could not build the world without matter. What! Has
God put into our hands the keys and the last resorts of his power? Is he
obliged not to exceed the limits of our knowledge? Take the case, oh
man, that you have been able to note here some traces of his acts: do
you think he has done all he could, and that he has put all his forms
and all his ideas into that work? You see only the order and the governance of that little cave where you are lodged, if you even see that; his
divinity has an infinite jurisdiction beyond that—this room is nothing
in comparison with the whole:

> . . . *all those things, with the heaven and the earth and the
> sea,*
> *Are nothing beside the sum of the sum of the whole of
> everything.*[174]

It is a local law you are invoking; you do not know what the universal
law is. Attach yourself to that to which you are subject, but not to him.
He is not your friend, your fellow citizen, or companion; if he commu-
nicates himself to you in any way, it is not to reduce himself to your pet-
tiness nor to give you control of his power. The human body cannot fly
to the clouds; that law is for you. The sun moves ceaselessly through its
regular course; the limits of the seas and the land cannot be confused;
water is unstable and without solidity; without breakage a wall is impenetrable to a solid body; man cannot preserve his life in the flames; he

172. 1 Corinthians 1:25.
173. See Diogenes Laertius, *Lives*, "Stilpon," II, 117.
174. Lucretius, *De rerum natura*, VI, 679–80.

cannot be both in the heavens and on the earth or bodily in a thousand places at once. It is for you that he has made these rules; it is you that they bind. He has borne witness to Christians that he has freed them all when it pleased him to do so. Truly, all powerful as he is, why would he have restrained his powers within a certain measure? In whose favor would he have renounced his privilege? Your reason has no more verisimilitude and no more foundation than in persuading you of the plurality of worlds:

> <That the earth, and the sun, the moon, the sea, and other
>   things that are
> Not one, but innumerable beyond number.>[175]

The most famous minds of past times believed it, as well as some from our own time, seemingly compelled by human reason. Especially since there is nothing unique and unified in this edifice we see,

> < . . . since in the whole there is not one thing
> That reproduces alone and grows by itself alone,>[176]

and that all species are multiplied in some number, from which it does not seem probable that God made this one work without companion, or that the matter of this form had been wholly exhausted in the one individual,

> <Wherefore again and again you must confess
> That there are here and there other gatherings of matter
> Such as this, which the ether holds in its tight grip,>[177]

notably if it is an animate being, as its movement makes credible, <<as Plato testifies, and as others of our people either confirm or do not dare deny; no more than that ancient opinion that the heavens, the stars, and other members of the world are creatures composed of body and soul, mortal in view of their composition, but immortal by the determination of the creator.>> But, if there are several worlds, as <<Democritus,>> Epicurus, and almost all philosophy have thought, how do we know if the rules of this one bear equally on the others? They may well have another visage and another governance. <<Epicurus imagines

175. Lucretius, De rerum natura, II, 1085–6.
176. Lucretius, De rerum natura, II, 1077–8.
177. Lucretius, De rerum natura, II, 1064–6.

them either similar or dissimilar.>> We see in this world an infinite difference and variety merely because of the distance between places. Neither grain nor wine is seen, nor any of our animals, in those new lands that our fathers discovered; everything there is different. <<And in the past, see in how many parts of the world neither Bacchus nor Ceres was known.>> If you want to believe Pliny <<or Herodotus,>> there are kinds of men in certain places who have very little resemblance to ours.

<And there are hybrid and ambiguous forms between human and brute nature. There are countries where the men are born without heads, carrying their eyes and mouth on the chest; where they are all androgynous; where they walk on four feet; where they have only one eye on the forehead, and the head more like a dog's than like ours; where they are half fishes in the lower part and live in the water; where the women give birth when they are five years old and live only eight; where they have the head and skin of the forehead so hard that iron cannot bite into it and bounces off it; where men have no beards; <<nations without the use or knowledge of fire; others who produce black sperm.>>

What, those who change naturally into wolves, <<into mares,>> and again into men? And if it is the case,> as Plutarch says, that in some place in the Indies there are men without a mouth, nourishing themselves from the scent of certain odors, how many of our descriptions are false? Man can no longer laugh nor perchance be capable of reason and of society. The governance and the cause of our internal structure would be for the most part irrelevant.

Besides, how many things are there of our acquaintance that resist the fine rules we have fashioned and prescribed to nature? And we undertake to attach God himself to them! How many things do we call miraculous and against nature? <<That is done by every man and by every nation according to the measure of their ignorance.>> How many occult properties and quintessences do we find? For to go according to nature, for us, is only to go according to our intelligence, insofar as we can follow and insofar as we can see into it. What is beyond is monstrous and disordered. But on this reckoning, for the most far-seeing and the cleverest, everything will therefore be monstrous—that is, for those people whom human reason has persuaded that they have neither any footing nor any foundation, not even just to assure them <<that snow is white (Anaxagoras said it was black); whether there is something or whether there is nothing; whether there is knowledge or ignorance (Metrodorus Chius denied that man could decide this);>> or whether we are alive—as Euripides is in doubt whether the life we are living is life or whether what we call death is life—

Who knows if what we call dying is not living,
As living is dying.[178]

<And this is not unlikely, for why do we assume the title of being from this instant, which is only a flash in the infinite course of an eternal night and so brief an interruption of our perpetual and natural condition? <<For death occupies all that is beyond and all that is before this moment and a good part of this moment as well.>> Others judge that there is no movement, that nothing budges, <<like all the followers of Melissus (for, if there is only one being, neither circular movement nor movement from one place to another can serve it, as Plato proves),>> that there is neither generation nor corruption in nature.>

<<Protagoras says there is nothing in nature but doubt; that one can dispute equally about all things, and about this too: whether one can dispute equally about all things. Nausiphanes: that of all things that seem, nothing is any more than it is not, that nothing is certain but uncertainty. Parmenides: that of all that seems, there is not anything in general, and that there is only one. Zeno: that even the one is not, and that there is nothing.

If one thing were, it would be either in another or in itself; if it is in another, there are two; if it is in itself, there are also two—the including and the included. According to these dogmas the nature of things is only a shadow, either false or vain.>>

It has always seemed to me that to a Christian this sort of talk is full of indiscretion and irreverence: God cannot die, God cannot deny himself, God cannot do this or that. I do not find it good thus to confine divine power within the laws of our speech. And what is offered to us in those propositions ought to be represented more reverently and more devoutly.

Our way of speaking has its weaknesses and its faults, like all the rest. Most of the occasions for the troubles of the world are grammatical. Our lawsuits arise only from debate about the interpretation of the laws, and most wars, from the failure to know clearly how to express the conventions and treaties of princes. How numerous and how important are the quarrels produced in the world by doubt about the meaning of this syllable: *hoc*! <Let us take the clause that logic itself will present as the clearest. If you say, "The weather is fine," and if you are speaking the truth, the weather is fine. Isn't that a way of speaking with certainty? Yet it will deceive you. That this is so, take an example: If you say, "I am lying," and if you are telling the truth, then you are lying. The art, the

178. Stobaeus, *Apophthegmata*, sermo 119.

reasoning, the force of the conclusion of this are the same as in the other case; nevertheless, there you are, bogged down.> I see the Pyrrhonian philosophers who cannot explain their general conception in any kind of discourse; for they would need a new language. Ours is formed wholly of affirmative propositions, which are entirely inimical to them. So that when they say, "I doubt," they are held to be running at the mouth for asserting that at least they avow and know that they doubt. Thus they are forced to save themselves by this comparison with medicine: when they assert, "I do not know," or "I doubt," they are saying that this proposition carries itself away, like all the rest, no more nor less than rhubarb, which evacuates the bad humors and itself at the same time.

<This idea is better conceived by asking, "What do I know?"—words I inscribe on the image of a pair of scales.>

See how we can guard ourselves against this kind of speech full of irreverence. With the disputes current in our religion, if you press the adversaries too hard, they will tell you quite roundly that it is not in God's power to have his body in paradise, and on earth, and in several places at once. And how that ancient mocker profits from this![179] At least, he says, it is no slight consolation to man when he sees that God cannot do everything; for God cannot kill himself when he wants to, which is the greatest privilege we have in our condition; God cannot make mortals immortal; nor revive the dead; nor bring it about that he who has lived has not lived or that he who has had honors has not had them, for God has no power over the past except forgetfulness. And, to tie this association of man with God to pleasant examples: he cannot keep twice ten from being twenty. That is what he says and what a Christian should not allow his mouth to utter, where, against the grain, it seems that men are experimenting with this mad arrogance of language in order to bring God to their measure,

> Let the father fill the heavens tomorrow
> With a black cloud or a pure sun; yet he will not
> Make invalid what has happened,
> Nor will he fashion differently and make undone
> What the fleeting hour has once brought.[180]

When we say that the infinity of centuries, past as well as future, is to God but an instant, or that his goodness, wisdom, power are the same thing as his essence, our speech says this, but our intelligence does not

179. Pliny was mentioned in the first edition. See Pliny, Naturalis historia, II, 7.
180. Horace, Odes, III, xxix, 43–8.

in the least apprehend it. And yet our presumptuousness wants to pass divinity through our sieve. And from this arise all the musings and errors with which the world finds itself taken, reducing and weighing on its scale a thing so distant from its own weight. <<*"It is amazing how far the arrogance of the human heart goes when the least little success encourages it."*[181]

How insolently the Stoics reprove Epicurus for holding that true well-being and happiness belong only to God and that the wise man has only a shadow and likeness of it!>> How boldly they have attached God to destiny (as, so far as I am concerned, no one called a Christian still does!), and Thales, Plato, and Pythagoras have subjected him to necessity! This pride in wanting to discover God with our eyes has brought it about that one of our prominent persons has given divinity a bodily form. <And that is why it happens to us every day that, by a particular assignment, we attribute to God events of special importance. Because they weigh on us, it seems that they weigh on him, too, and that he looks at these more completely and attentively than at events of less weight for us and with more ordinary consequences.> <<*"The gods care about big things, and neglect little ones."*[182] Hear Cicero's example; he will give you his reason: *"Nor do kings care about all the little details of their reign."*[183]

As if it were more or less difficult for him to move an empire or the leaf of a tree, and as if providence worked differently when shaping the outcome of a battle than the leap of a flea! The hand of his government extends to all things in the same way, with the same force and the same order; our interest has nothing to do with it; our activities and our standards do not touch it.

"God is a great artificer in great things, as he is not a lesser in small ones."[184] Our arrogance always sets us before this impious comparison. Because our preoccupations weigh us down, Strato has given immunity from all offices to the gods as well as to their priests. He has all things produced and maintained by nature, and constructs the parts of the world from its weight and movements, freeing human nature from all fear of divine judgments. *"What is blessed and eternal, does not have to make any transactions or make a display for anyone."*[185] Nature wants

181. Pliny, *Naturalis historia*, II, 23.
182. Cicero, *De natura deorum*, II, xlvi.
183. Cicero, *De natura deorum*, II, xxxv.
184. Cicero, *De natura deorum*, II, lvi.
185. Cicero, *De natura deorum*, I, xvii.

like relations in like things. Thus the infinite number of mortals implies a like number of immortals. The infinite things that kill and injure presuppose as many that preserve and profit. As the souls of the gods, without tongues, without eyes, without ears, feel among themselves what the other feels, and judge our thoughts: so the souls of men, when they are free and separated from the body through sleep or some enchantment, divine, prognosticate, and see things they would not know how to see if they were mixed with bodies.>>

Men, says Saint Paul, have gone mad, believing they are wise; and they have changed the glory of God, who is incorruptible, into the image of corruptible man.

<Look for a moment at this juggling of ancient deifications. After the great and proud pomp of burial, as the fire came to reach the apex of the pyramid and caught the bed of the departed, at the same time they let fly an eagle, which, flying aloft, signified that the soul was going to paradise. We have a thousand medals, and notably of that fine woman Faustina, where the eagle is represented carrying those deified souls limply on its back. It is too bad that we trick ourselves with our own monkey business and inventions—

What they have made, they fear,[186]

—as children are frightened by the very face of their playmates whom they have daubed and darkened. <<*"Who is unhappier than a man whom his fictions govern?"*[187] It is far better to honor him who has made us than to honor the one we have made.>> Augustus had more temples than Jupiter, served with as much worship and belief in miracles. The Thasians, in recompense for the benefits they had received from Agesilaus, came to tell him they had canonized him. "Does your nation," he asked them, "have the power to make into God whomever it likes? As an example, make a god of one among you, and then <<when I have seen how he gets on,>> I will thank you very much for your offer."

<<Man is quite mad. He does not know how to produce a mite and produces gods by the dozens.

Hear Trismegistus praise our adequacy. Of all wonderful things, one has surpassed wonder itself: the fact that man has been able to find and to make the divine nature exceeds all admirable things.>>

These are the arguments of the school of philosophy itself,

186. Lucan, *Pharsalia*, I, 486.
187. Pliny, *Naturalis historia*, II, 7.

*To whom alone it is given to know the gods and celestial
    powers,*
Or to know nothing.[188]

If God exists, he is animate; if he is animate, he has senses; and if he has
senses, he is subject to corruption. If he is without body, he is without
soul and consequently without action; and if he has body, he is perish-
able. Isn't that a triumph?

   <<We are incapable of having made the world. Thus there is some
more excellent nature that has put its hand to it.—It would be stupid
arrogance of us to consider ourselves the most perfect thing in this universe; thus there is something better; that is God.—When you see a
rich and formal dwelling, even if you do not know who is its master, still
you will not say it was built for rats. And as to that divine structure of the
celestial palace that we see, do we not have to believe that it is the resi-
dence of some master greater than we are? Is not the highest always the
most worthy? And we are placed at the bottom.—Nothing without soul
and without reason can produce a living being capable of reason. The
world produces us; therefore it has soul and reason.—Every part of us is
less than we are. We are part of the world; thus the world is supplied
with wisdom and reason, and more abundantly than we are.—It is a
fine thing to have a great government. So the government of the world
belongs to some fortunate nature.—The stars do not give any trouble;
thus they are full of benevolence.>>—We need nourishment; thus the
gods do, too, and feed on exhalations from down here. <<Earthly goods
are not goods for God; therefore they are not goods for us.—To offend
and to be offended are equally evidences of imbecility; thus it is folly to
fear God.—God is good by his nature, man, by his industry, which is
more.—Divine wisdom and human wisdom have no other distinction
but that the former is eternal. But duration is no supplement to wisdom; hence we are companions.>>—We have life, reason, and liberty;
we value goodness, charity, and justice; therefore these qualities are in
him. In short, construction and destruction, the conditions of divinity,
are made by man, according to man's relation to himself. What a
patron, and what a model! Extend, elevate, and enlarge human qualities as much as we please; inflate yourself, poor man! And yet, and yet,
and yet,

    Not if you should burst, he said.[189]

188. Lucan, *Pharsalia*, I, 452–3.
189. Horace, *Odes*, II, iii, 318.

<<"*Certainly men, when they try to think of God, whom they cannot conceive of, conceive only of themselves; they compare him to themselves, and not themselves to him.*">>[190]

In natural things, the effects refer only partially to their causes: What is this thing? It is beyond the order of nature; its condition is too lofty, too far away, and too dominating to allow our conclusions to attach it and pin it down. It is not through us that you arrive; that route is too lowly. We are no closer to the heavens on top on Mount Senis than at the bottom of the sea: to see this, consult your astrolabe. They reduce God to the carnal knowledge of women, how many times, in how many generations? Paulina, the wife of Saturninus, a matron with a high reputation in Rome, when she thought she was sleeping with the god Serapis found herself in the arms of a lover of hers through the pandering of that temple's priests.

<<Varro, the subtlest and most learned Latin author, writes in the books of his *Theology* that the sacristan of Hercules, drawing lots, with one hand for himself, the other for Hercules, played against him for a supper and a girl: if he won, it would be at the expense of the offerings; if he lost, at his own expense. He lost, and paid for his supper and his girl. Her name was Laurentina; at night she saw that god in her arms telling her, moreover, that the first person she would meet in the morning would pay her wages in heavenly fashion. This was Taruntius, a rich young man who took her home with him and in time made her his heir. She, in her turn, hoping to do something agreeable to that god, made the Roman people her heir, for which reason they give her divine honors.

As if it were not enough that Plato was descended from the gods on both sides and had Neptune as the common ancestor of his line, it was considered certain at Athens that Ariston, who wanted to enjoy the lovely Perictione, but could not, was warned in a dream by the god Apollo to leave her untarnished and intact until she had given birth; those were Plato's father and mother. How often is it, in stories, that such cuckoldries are achieved by the gods against unfortunate human beings, and husbands injuriously discredited in favor of their children?

In the religion of Mohammed there are plenty of Merlins to be found, according to the people's belief, that is to say, children without a father, spiritually—indeed divinely—in the womb of virgins; and they have a name that has that meaning in their language.>>

We must take note that for everything, nothing is more precious and more estimable than its own being <<(the lion, the eagle, the dolphin

---

190. Saint Augustine, *City of God*, XII, xvii.

rate nothing higher than their own species);>> and that each one relates the qualities of all other things to its own qualities, which we may well extend and reduce, but that is all; for our imagination cannot reach beyond that relation and that principle. It cannot conjecture anything else or go beyond that limit. <<Where do those old arguments come from: Of all forms, the fairest is man's; thus God has that form. No one can be happy without virtue, nor can virtue exist without reason, and reason can lodge nowhere but in the human shape; therefore God is clothed in human shape.

"Such is the molding, the prejudice, of our minds, that to man, when he thinks of a god, it is the human form that occurs.">>[191]

Yet Xenophanes said jokingly that if animals create gods, as it is probable that they do, they certainly create them in their own image and glorify them, as we do. For why won't a gosling say this: "All the parts of the universe concern me; the earth serves me for walking, the sun to give me light, the stars to breathe into me their influences; I have such and such comfort from the winds, such from the waters; there is nothing that that vault looks on as favorably as it does me; I am the beloved of nature; isn't it man who looks after me, houses me, waits on me? It is for me that he sows and reaps; if he eats me, he also eats man, his companion, and so do I eat the worms that kill him and eat him." A crane could say as much on the subject, and still more magnificently for the freedom of its flights and the possession of that lovely and lofty region: <<*"For so smooth, so conciliatory, such a bawd is nature to herself."*>>[192]

But then, by the same train of thought, for us are the fates, for us the world; it shines, it thunders for us; both creator and creatures, everything is for us. This is the end and the point at which the universality of things aim. Consider the account that philosophy has given, for two thousand years and more, of celestial matters: the gods have acted, have spoken, only for man; it attributes to them no other concern and no other vocation. Here they are at war against us:

> . . . *and the children of the earth,*
> *Tamed by the hand of Hercules,*
> *Wherefore the fair palace of old Saturn*
> *Trembled at the peril.*[193]

191. Cicero, *De natura deorum*, I, xxvii.
192. Cicero, *De natura deorum*, I, xxvii.
193. Horace, *Odes*, II, xii, 6–9.

There they are, partisans of our troubles, <<to repay us in kind for the fact that so many times we are their partisans:>>

> *Making the walls tremble with his great trident,*
> *Neptune overturns them and lays low the city.*
> *Cruelest Juno is near the Scean gates,*
> *In first place there.*[194]

<<The Caunians, out of jealousy for the domination of their own gods, arm themselves on the day of their devotion and go running through all the precincts of their city, beating the air here and there with their swords, driving off and banishing strange gods from their territory.>> Their powers are restricted according to our needs: one cures horses, one, men; <<one, the plague;>> one, the ringworm; one, the cough, <<one, one kind of itch, one, another (*"thus bad religion introduces the gods even into the smallest things"*);>>[195] one makes the grapes grow, another, garlic; one is in charge of lechery; one, of trade <<(there is a god for every kind of artisan);>> one has his province and reputation in the east; one, in the west:

> *. . . here were her arms,*
> *There was her chariot.*[196]

> <<*Oh, sacred Apollo, you who hold the sure navel of the earth!*[197]

> *To the Athenians, Pallas; to Diana, Minoan Crete,*
> *Hypsipilus to Vulcan. For Juno,*
> *Peloponnesian Sparta and also Mycenae.*
> *Faunus to Mount Menalus with its pine woods.*
> *Mars is to be worshipped in Latium.*>>[198]

One has only a small town or a family in his possession; <<one lives alone; another in company, whether voluntarily or by necessity.

> *The ancestors' temple adjoins those of the descendant.* >>[199]

194. Virgil, *Aeneid*, II, 610–3.
195. Livy, *Histories*, XXVII, xxxiii.
196. Virgil, *Aeneid*, I, 16–7.
197. Cicero, *De divinatione*, II, xvi.
198. Ovid, *Fasti*, III, 81–4.
199. Ovid, *Fasti*, I, 294.

There are some so wretched and vulgar (for their number reaches 36,000), that five or six have to be accumulated to produce a grain of wheat, and they take their different names from this; <<it takes three for a door: one for the board, one for the hinge pin, one for the threshold; four for an infant: protectors of its swaddling clothes, its drink, its food, its suckling; some certain, some uncertain and doubtful; some who do not yet enter into Paradise—

> Even if we refuse them the honor of heaven,
> Let us keep for them the land that receives each of them[200]

—there are among them scientists, poets, civilians; some halfway between divine and human nature, mediators, negotiators between us and God, worshipped by a second, diminutive order of worship; infinite in titles and ceremonies; some good, others bad.>> Some of them are old and broken, and some are mortal; for Chrysippus estimates that at the last conflagration of the world all the gods would have to perish except Jupiter. <<Man creates a thousand pleasant associations between God and himself. Is he not God's compatriot?

> Crete, cradle of Jupiter.[201]

Here is the excuse that Scevola, great pontiff, and Varro, great theologian, give us about this subject in their time: that there is need for the people to be ignorant of many true things and believe many false ones: "since he seeks the truth in order to be liberated, one can also believe that it is good for him to be deceived."->>[202]

Human eyes cannot see things except through the forms of our knowledge. <<And we forget what a fall the miserable Phaeton took because he wanted to manage the reins of his father's horses with a mortal hand. Our mind sinks to the same depth, vanishes, and is bruised in the same way through its temerity.>> If you ask philosophy of what stuff are the heavens and the sun, what would it answer you if not of iron, or <<with Anaxagoras,>> of stone, or of such stuff as we use? <<If you ask Zeno what nature is, he says "a fire, an artisan, able to engender, proceeding according to rule.">> Archimedes, master of that science which claims precedence over all the others in truth and certainty: "The sun," he says, "is a god of fiery iron." Isn't that a fine

---

200. Ovid, *Metamorphoses*, I, 194–5.
201. Ovid, *Metamorphoses*, VIII, 99.
202. Saint Augustine, *City of God*, IV, xxxi.

image produced by the beauty and inevitable necessity of geometric demonstrations? Yet not so inevitable <<and useful>> but that <<Socrates thought all you needed to know was enough geometry to be able to measure the earth you bought and sold, and>> that Polyaenus, who had been a famous and illustrious geometer, held it in contempt, as full of falsity and obvious vanity, after he had tasted the sweet fruits of the languorous gardens of Epicurus.>

<<Socrates, in Xenophon, concerning this proposal of Anaxagoras, who was supposed by antiquity learned beyond all other celestial and divine beings, says that he is troubled in his brain, as are all men who pursue immoderately the knowledge of things that lie beyond their appearance. When he made the sun a burning stone, he did not consider that a stone does not shine in the fire and, worse, that it is consumed there; in his uniting the sun and the fire, that fire does not blacken those who look at it; that we look firmly at fire; that fire kills plants and grasses. According to the opinion of Socrates, and according to mine also, to judge most wisely about the sun is not to judge at all.

Plato, before speaking of the *daimons* in the *Timaeus*: "It is an enterprise that exceeds our range. We have to believe the ancients who said they were begotten by them. It is against reason to refuse credence to the children of the gods, even when what they say is not established by necessary and probable arguments, since they reply to us by speaking of things relating to home and family.">>

Let us see if we have a bit more clarity in the knowledge of human and natural things.

Is it not a ridiculous enterprise to go and create another body and to give a false form of our invention to those things which, by our own confession, our science cannot reach: as we see in the movement of the planets, to which we lend from ourselves heavy, bodily, and material mechanisms, insofar as our mind cannot reach or imagine their natural behavior:

> . . . *the shaft was golden, and the wheels*
> *Had golden circles above and the row of spikes was silver.*[203]

You will say that we have had coachmen, carpenters <<and painters>> who have gone up there to make engines with motions <<and to arrange the wheels and interlacings of the celestial bodies, variegated in color around the spindle of necessity, according to Plato:>>

---

203. Ovid, *Metamorphoses*, II, 107–8.

<The world, a mansion, is the greatest of beings;
Five zones on its borders form a sublime circle.
A gleaming headband, which carries twelve signs,
Radiating from the stars, obliquely cuts the ether,
And there the moon drives its chariot with two horses.[204]

These are all dreams and fanatical follies. That it may one day please nature to open its bosom to us and make us see for ourselves the means and workings of its movements, and prepare our eyes for it! Oh, God! What abuses, what errors we would find in our poor science:> <<I am mistaken if it has a single thing correctly in its focus, and I will leave here more ignorant of everything except my ignorance.

Have I not seen in Plato that divine word, that nature is nothing but an enigmatic poem—as one might perhaps say it was a veiled and shadowy painting, glimmering with an infinite variety of false lights to stimulate our conjectures?

"All things are hidden and covered with thick darkness, and there is no mind incisive enough to penetrate into the heavens or enter beneath the earth."[205]

And certainly philosophy is nothing but sophisticated poetry. Where do those ancient authors get their authorities except from the poets? The first of them were themselves poets and they treated philosophy in their art form. Plato is only an incoherent poet. Timon calls him, insultingly, a great maker of miracles.>>

Just as women use ivory teeth where their own are lacking, and, instead of their true complexion, create one from some foreign matter; as they make themselves thighs of cloth and felt, and fullness of figure with cotton, and in plain sight of everyone embellish themselves with a false and borrowed beauty: so does science <(and even our law, they say, has legitimate fictions on which it founds the truth of its justice).> It gives us in payment, and in principle the things that it itself teaches us are invented, for, as to those epicycles, eccentrics, concentrics with which astrology helps itself guide the burning of its stars, it gives them to us as the best it has been able to invent on this subject; similarly, in other matters philosophy presents to us not what is or what it believes, but what it creates that has more plausibility and graciousness. <<Plato on what is said about the state of our body and that of beasts: "We would assert that what we have said is true, if we had on this the confirmation

---

204. Varro, from Probus' commentary on Virgil, *Eclogues*, VI.

205. Cicero, *Academica*, II, xxxix.

of an oracle; we can only assert that it is the most likely to be true of what we have been able to say.">>

It is not only to the heavens that philosophy sends its ropes, its engines, and its wheels. Consider for a bit what it says about ourselves and our fabric. There is no more retrogradation, trepidation, accession, backing up, carrying off in the stars and celestial bodies than they have created in this poor little human body. Indeed, in view of that, they were right to call it the microcosm, so many pieces and aspects have they employed to put it together and build it. To accommodate the movements they see in man, the different functions and faculties they notice in us, into how many parts have they divided our soul? In how many seats have they lodged it? Into how many orders and stages have they divided that poor man, besides those that are natural and perceptible? And into how many duties and activities? They make of it an imaginary republic. It is a subject they hold and handle: they are granted every power to rip it open, arrange it, reassemble it, and fill it out, each according to his fancy; and still they do not possess it. Not only in truth, but even in dreams they cannot regulate it, so that there is not some cadence or some sound that escapes their design, prodigious though it is, and patched together of a thousand false and fantastic pieces. <<And that is no reason to excuse them. For, as to painters, when they paint the sky, the earth, the seas, the mountains, faraway islands, we forgive them for giving us only some hint, and, as with unknown things, we are satisfied with some shadow and pretense or other. But when they draw after nature on a subject that is familiar and known to us, we demand of them a perfect and exact representation of lineaments and colors, and we hold it against them if they fail.>>

I gladly acknowledge the Milesian girl who, seeing the philosopher Thales constantly amusing himself in the contemplation of the celestial vault and always keeping his eyes upward, put in his way something to make him stumble to show him that it would be time to amuse himself with things in the clouds when he had provided for those at his feet. She was certainly giving him good advice in telling him to look rather at himself than at the heavens. <<For, as Democritus said through the voice of Cicero,

> No one looks at what is under his feet; they look at the
> regions of the sky.>>[206]

But our condition brings it about that the knowledge of what we have between our hands is as far from us and even as far beyond the clouds

206. Cicero, *De divinatione*, II, xiii.

as is the knowledge of the stars. <<As Socrates says in Plato, one may make the same reproach that woman made to Thales to anyone who meddles with philosophy: that he sees nothing of what is in front of him. For every philosopher is ignorant of what his neighbor is doing, yes, and of what he is doing himself and is ignorant of what they both are, whether beasts or men.>>

Those people who find Sebond's arguments too weak, who are ignorant of nothing, who govern the world, who know everything—

> What causes calm the sea; what regulates the year;
> Whether the stars move and wander of themselves or by
>   command;
> What produces the darkness of the moon, what brings forth
>   its orb;
> What makes possible the discordant harmony of things?[207]

—have they not sometimes pondered among their books the difficulties they met with in understanding their own being? We do indeed see that the finger is moving, that the foot is moving; that some parts bestir themselves without our leave and that we perturb others at our own command; that a certain apprehension produces blushing, another, pallor; a certain imagination acts only in the spleen, another, in the brain; one produces laughter, the other, tears; another affects and astonishes all our senses, and stops the movement of our limbs. <<At such an object the stomach rises; and at another, some part lower down.>> But how a mental impression makes such a breach on a massive and solid subject, and the nature of the relation and the linkage of these marvelous devices, man has never known. <<"*All things are uncertain to reason and hidden in the majesty of nature,*" says Pliny.[208] And Saint Augustine: "*The way in which minds adhere to bodies is wholly wonderful, nor can it be understood by man; and yet this very thing is man.*">>[209] All the same, this is never subject to doubt, for men's opinions are received following ancient beliefs, by authority and upon trust, as if it were religion or law. We receive what is commonly held as if it were everyday parlance; we receive this truth with all its superstructure and attachments of arguments and proofs, like a firm and solid body that can no longer be shaken, that can no longer be judged. On the contrary, everyone, in competition with everyone else,

207. Horace, *Epistles*, I, xii, 16–9.
208. Pliny, *Naturalis historia*, II, xxxvii.
209. Saint Augustine, *City of God*, XXI, x.

goes on smoothing over and strengthening that received belief as far as his reason can—a supple instrument that can be turned about and adapted to every shape. Thus the world fills itself and comforts itself with insipidity and lies.

The reason we scarcely doubt about things is that we never test common impressions; we don't look where our feet are or where the fault or the weakness lies; we debate only the branches; we do not ask if that is true, but whether it has been understood in this or that way. We do not ask if Galen said anything worthwhile, but whether he said it this way or otherwise. Indeed, there was good reason for this bridle and constraint on the freedom of our judgment and this tyranny over our beliefs to extend to the schools and to the arts. The god of scholastic knowledge is Aristotle; it is religion to debate about his ordinances, as it is for those of Lycurgus at Sparta. His doctrine, which can just as well be false as any other, serves us as magisterial law. I don't know why I should not accept just as willingly the ideas of Plato or the atoms of Epicurus, the fullness and void of Lucretius and Democritus, the water of Thales, Anaximander's infinity of nature, the air of Diogenes, the numbers and symmetry of Pythagoras, the infinite of Parmenides, the one of Musaeus, the water and fire of Apollodorus, the similar parts of Anaxagoras, the love and hate of Empedocles, the fire of Heraclitus, or every other opinion of that infinite confusion of judgments and of propositions that our fair human reason produces through its certainty and clairvoyance in everything it meddles with, as I should the opinion of Aristotle on this subject of the principles of natural things: principles that he builds of three parts, matter, form, and privation. And what is more useless than to make inanity itself the cause of the production of things? Privation is a negative; out of what whimsy was he able to make it the cause and origin of the things that are? However, no one would dare to question this except as an exercise in logic. Nothing is debated to cast doubt on it, but only to defend the author of the school from strange objections; his authority is the end beyond which it is not permitted to inquire.

It is very easy to build whatever one wants on avowed foundations, for according to the law and ordinance of this beginning, the rest of the parts of the building are easily managed without self-contradiction. In this way we find our reasoning well-founded and we discourse with the end in sight; for, through their explicit demands, in the fashion of geometers, our masters already occupy and gain ahead of time as much space in our belief as they need to reach whatever conclusions they want. The consent and approbation we lend them gives them the means to pull us to the left or right and to turn us round in circles at their will. Whoever is believed as to his presuppositions is our master and our god; he will make the planting of his foundations so broad and so simple that through them we can rise to the clouds if he likes. In the practice and business of knowledge we have taken for sound currency the word of Pythagoras that every expert must be believed in his own specialty. The dialectician appeals to the grammarian on the meaning of words; the rhetorician borrows from the dialectician the modes of argument; the poet borrows measures from the musician; the geometer, proportions from the arithmetician; metaphysicians take for their foundation the conjectures of physics. For each science has its pre-established principles by which human judgment is bridled on all sides. If you try to break that barrier where the chief error lies, they at once mouth that sentence: that it is impossible to argue against those who deny the principles.

But there cannot be any principles for human beings if divinity has not revealed those principles to them; of all the rest—the beginning, the middle, and the end—there is only dream and smoke. For those who argue by presuppositions, one must presuppose, on the contrary, the very axiom about which one is arguing. For every human presupposition and pronouncement has as much authority as every other if it is only reason that makes the difference. Thus we must put them all on the balance, and first the general ones and those that tyrannize over us. <<The impression of certainty is certain evidence of madness and extreme uncertainty; there are no people madder, no less the philosophers than Plato's philodoxists.[210]>> It is necessary to know if fire is hot, if snow is white, if there is anything hard or soft within our knowledge.

And as to those replies of which old stories are made—like the one to the person who doubted fire, that he should throw himself into it; to the person who denied that ice was cold, that he should put some on his bosom—those replies are most unworthy of the profession of philosophy. If they had left us in our natural state, receiving strange appearances according to how they presented themselves to us through our senses, and had let us follow our simple appetites, which are governed by our condition at birth, they would have reason to speak to us; but it is from them we have learned to make ourselves judges of the world; it is from them we get this fancy: that human reason is general governor of everything outside or inside the celestial vault, and that it embraces everything, can do anything, and by means of it everything knows and acknowledges itself.

210. Plato contrasts philodoxists, lovers of opinion, with philosophers, lovers of wisdom.

This reply would be good among the cannibals, who enjoy the bless-
ing of a long, peaceful, and quiet life without the precepts of Aristotle
and without knowing the name of physics.[211] This reply might be worth
more and could have more solidity than all that they could borrow from
their reason and their ingenuity. On this ground all the animals would
be as capable as we are, and so would everything where the command of
natural law is still pure and simple; but they have renounced it. They do
not have to tell me: "It is true, for you see and sense it this way;" they
have to tell me that what I think I sense, I do in fact sense; and if I sense
it, they have to tell me afterward why I sense it, and how, and what; they
have to tell me the name, the origin, the ins and outs of heat, of cold, the
qualities of what acts and what is acted on. Or let them quit their profession, which is to receive or approve nothing except through the path of
reason; that is their touchstone for every kind of undertaking, but surely
it is a touchstone full of falsity, of error or weakness and failure.

How do we want to test it better than through itself? If it is not to be
believed when speaking of itself, it will scarcely be fit to judge of foreign things; if it knows anything, this will at least be its being and its
dwelling place. It is in the soul and, in fact, part or effect of it: for what
is essential is true reason, which we rob of its name on false authority.
It dwells in the bosom of God. It has there its resting place and its
retreat. It is from there that it comes when it pleases God to let us see
some ray of it, as Pallas sprang from the head of her father to communicate with the world.

So let us see what human reason has taught us about itself and the
soul, <<not about the soul in general, in which almost all philosophy
makes the heavenly bodies and the first bodies participate, nor of the
soul that Thales attributed even to the things we consider inanimate,
convinced by consideration of the magnet, but of the soul that belongs
to us, which we must know better:>>

> <*For they do not know the nature of the soul,*
> *Whether it is born, or finds its way into them at birth,*
> *And whether it perishes with us when death tears us apart,*
> *Or visits the shades of Orcas and his vast pools,*
> *Or by divine will enters into other beings?>*[212]

To Crates and Dicaearchus, it was clear that there was nothing in it at
all, but that the body bestirs itself in this way by a natural motion; to

---

211. See also Montaigne, *Essays*, I, 31, "On Cannibals."
212. Lucretius, *De rerum natura*, I, 113–7.

Plato, that it was a substance moving of itself; to Thales, a nature without rest; to Asclepiades, an activity of the senses; to Hesiod and Anaximander, a thing composed of earth and water; to Parmenides, of earth and fire; to Empedocles, of blood—

> *He vomits his bloody soul*[213]

—to Posidonius, Cleanthes, and Galen, heat or a hot complexion—

> *Their vigor is of heat, and its origin in the heavens*[214]

—to Hippocrates, a spirit spread through the body; to Varro, air received through the mouth, heated in the lungs, tempered in the heart, and spread through the whole body; to Zeno, the quintessence of the four elements; to Heraclides Ponticus, light; to Xenocrates and the Egyptians, a moveable number; to the Chaldeans, a virtue without determinate form,

> <*. . . a certain vital habit of the body,*
> *Which the Greeks call a harmony.*>[215]

Let us not forget Aristotle: what naturally makes the body move, which he calls entelechy—as cold an invention as any other, for he speaks neither of the essence, nor of the origin, nor of the nature of the soul, but only of the effect. Lactantius, Seneca, and most of the dogmatists have admitted that this was something they did not understand. <<And after all that enumeration of opinions: "*Which one is true among these pronouncements, some god will see,*" says Cicero.>>[216] I know of my own knowledge, says Saint Bernard, how incomprehensible God is, since I cannot understand the parts of my own being. <<Heraclitus, who thought all being was full of souls and of *daimons,* nevertheless maintained that one could not advance far enough toward the knowledge of the soul to achieve it, so profound was its essence.>>

There is no less disagreement and debate about the seat of the soul. Hippocrates and Hierophilus put it in the cerebral ventricle; Democritus and Aristotle, in the whole body—

213. Virgil, *Aeneid,* IX, 349.
214. Virgil, *Aeneid,* VI, 730.
215. Lucretius, *De rerum natura,* III, 100–1.
216. Cicero, *Tusculan Disputations,* I, ii.

<It is often said that health is of the body,
And yet health is not a part of the body>[217]

—Epicurus, in the stomach—

<Here fear and terror throb, around these places
Joys palpitate.>[218]

   The Stoics, around and in the heart; Erasistratus, joining the membrane of the scalp; Empedocles, in the blood; so also Moses, which was the reason he forbade eating the blood of animals, to which their soul is joined; Galen thought that each part of the body had its soul; Strato placed it between the two eyebrows. <<*"What the soul looks like and where it lives, that is what must not be asked,"* says Cicero.[219] I willingly leave that man his own words. Would I go and alter his speech for eloquence? Besides, there is not much to be gained by hiding the matter of his inventions: they are neither very frequent, nor very rigid, nor are they unknown.>> But the reason Chrysippus, like the others of his sect, argues that it is around the heart is not to be forgotten: "It is for this reason," he says, "that when we want to certify something, we put our hand on the stomach; and when we want to say *ego*, which means me, we let the jaw fall toward the stomach." We cannot leave this subject without noticing the inanity of so great a person. For, apart from the fact that these considerations are very lightweight, the last could only prove to the Greeks that they have the soul in that place. There is no human judgment, however alert, that does not sometimes sleep.
   <<What are we afraid to say? Here are the Stoics, fathers of human prudence, who find that man's soul, caught under a ruin, pulls and pants a long time to get out, not being able to get rid of the burden, like a mouse caught in a trap.
   Some hold that the world was made to give a body, as punishment, to spirits that had fallen by their own fault from the purity in which they were created, while the first creation had been only incorporeal; and that they were more or less lightly or heavily embodied, according to their degree of distance from spirituality; hence the variety of so much of created matter. But the spirit that was, as its penalty, invested with the body of the sun, had to have a very rare and particular measure of change. The extremes of our inquiry all dazzle us: as Plutarch says of

217. Lucretius, *De rerum natura*, III, 103–4.
218. Lucretius, *De rerum natura*, III, 142–3.
219. Cicero, *Tusculan Disputations*, I, xviii.

the onset of histories, that in the same way as maps the edge of known lands is taken up with marshes, deep forests, deserts, and uninhabitable places. That is why the crudest and most childish ravings are found chiefly in those who treat things that are higher and more advanced and lose themselves in their curiosity and presumption. The end and the beginning of knowledge remain equally foolish. Watch Plato's flight ascend to his poetic clouds; see in him the jargon of the gods. But what was he dreaming of when>> he defined man as an animal with two feet and without feathers, giving those who wanted to make fun of him a pleasant occasion—for when they had plucked a live capon, they called it Plato's man.

And what about the Epicureans? How simple were they when they imagined, in the first place, that their atoms, which they said were bodies having some weight and a natural movement downward, had built the world—until they were informed by their adversaries that on this description, it would not be possible for the atoms to join and take hold of one another, their fall being thus straight and perpendicular and everywhere producing parallel lines? For that reason they had to add a sideways, random motion afterward, as well as to provide their atoms with curved and twisted tails to make them able to attach and unite themselves to one another.

<<And even then, don't those who pursue them with this further consideration give them trouble? If by lot the atoms are formed in so many different shapes, why have they never joined to make a house or a shoe? Why not even believe that an infinite number of Greek letters tossed around the place would suffice to arrive at the structure of the *Iliad*? What is capable of reason, says Zeno, is better than what is not capable of it; there is nothing better than the world, therefore the world is capable of reason. Cotta, by this same argument, makes the world a mathematician, and he makes it a musician and organist by another argument, also of Zeno's: "The whole is more than the part; we are capable of wisdom and are parts of the world; thus the world is wise.">>

Countless similar examples, not merely false, but inept arguments, which do not hold up at all and accuse their authors not so much of ignorance as of imprudence, are to be found in the reproaches that philosophers make to one another on the disagreements of their opinions and their sects. <<Anyone who would botch together sufficiently a collection of human asininities would be saying wonderful things.

I gladly collect some of them as a display, no less useful to consider, from a certain perspective, than sane and moderate opinions.>> In this way let us judge what we are to think of man, of his sense and his reason, since in those great figures who have so elevated human self-conceit we find such obvious and gross deficiencies. As for me, I prefer to think that they have been treating knowledge casually, like a toy in everyone's hands, and have played with reason as with a vain and frivolous instrument, putting forward all sorts of inventions and ideas, sometimes tighter, sometimes looser. That same Plato who defines man as a chicken says elsewhere, following Socrates, that he doesn't truly know what a man is, and that this is one of the parts of the world most difficult to know. Through this variety and instability of opinions they lead us by the hand, tacitly, to the resolution of their irresolution. By profession they do not always present their view openly and clearly. They have sometimes hidden it under the fabulous clouds of poetry, sometimes under some other mask—for our imperfection also includes the fact that raw meat does not always agree with our stomachs: it has to be dried, altered, and corrupted. They do the same: they sometimes obscure their naïve opinions and judgments and falsify them in order to accommodate themselves to public usage. They do not want to profess expressly the ignorance and imbecility of human reason <<for fear of frightening the children,>> but they make it plain enough to us under the appearance of troubled and inconstant knowledge.

<In Italy, I advised someone who was having trouble speaking Italian that as long as he was only trying to make himself understood and did not want to excel in other ways, he should just use the first words that came into his head—Latin, French, Spanish, or Gascon—adding the Italian ending; he could never fail to hit upon some idiom of the country, whether Tuscan, or Roman, or Venetian, or Piedmontese, or Neapolitan, and was bound to fasten on one of so many different forms. I say the same of philosophy: it has so many faces and varieties and has said so much that all our dreams and reveries are to be found in it. Human fancy cannot conceive of anything good or evil that is not contained there. <<"Nothing can be said so absurd that it is not said by some philosopher.">>[220] And I let my caprices go more freely in public, since, although they were engendered in me and without patron, I know they will find their kinship to some ancient humor, and there will always be someone to say: "That's where he gets it from!">

<<My habits are natural; to establish them, I have in no way invoked the help of any discipline. But silly as they are, when the wish has come over me to give an account of them and when, to make them appear a bit more decently in public, I took on myself the task of assisting them with arguments and cases, it was amazing even to myself to find them,

220. Cicero, *De divinatione*, II, lxviii.

as if by chance, in harmony with so many philosophical examples and arguments. It was only after my life had been used and spent that I learned what regimen it belonged to.

A new figure: an unpremeditated and accidental philosopher!>>

To return to our soul: when Plato put reason in the brain, anger in the heart, and greed in the liver, it was probably rather an interpretation of the movements of the soul than a division and separation that he wanted to make, as of a body with several limbs. And the most probable of these opinions is that it is always one soul that, through its faculties, reasons, remembers, understands, judges, desires, and exercises all its other operations through various instruments of the body (as the pilot directs his ship according to his experience, now tightening or loosening a rope, now hoisting the lateen yard or plying the oars, leading to different results through a single power)—and that it is located in the brain—which is clear from the fact that injuries and accidents affecting that part are extremely detrimental to the faculties of the soul. From there, it is not difficult for it to flow out to the rest of the body—

> <<Phoebus never deviates from his celestial path;
> Yet he illuminates all things with his rays>>[221]

—as the sun spreads out its light and its powers from the sky, and fills the world with them,

> <The other part of the soul, spread through the whole body,
> Obeys, and is moved at the will and inclination of the
> mind.>[222]

Some have said that there is a general soul, like a large body, from which all particular souls were derived and to which they would return, always mixing into that universal matter—

> . . . for God moves through all things,
> The earth and the bosom of the sea and the depth of the sky;
> From him cattle, herds, human beings, every kind of beast,
> Everything borrows at its birth the subtle breath of life.
> Then all returns to him, in him all is resolved.
> There is no place for death.[223]

221. Claudian, On the Sixth Consulate, V, 411–2.
222. Lucretius, De rerum natura, III, 144–5.

Others say that souls only joined and reattached themselves to it; others, that they were produced by the divine substance; others, by angels, by fire, and by air. Some, that they were produced long ago; some, at the very hour of need. Some have them descend from the circle of the moon and return to it. Most of the ancients said they were produced by the father in the son, in a similar manner and process as all other natural things, arguing for this from the resemblance of children to their fathers—

> Your father in begetting you instilled in you his virtue . . .
> The strong are created by the strong and good.[224]

—and from the fact that we see running from fathers to children not only physical marks, but humors, complexions, and inclinations of the soul—

> Again, why does fiery passion follow the grim brood of lions,
> Why is cunning given to foxes and flight to deer by their
>   fathers
> So that the father's fear incites their limbs,
> Unless because a certain power of mind
> Grows in its seed and stock at the same time as the whole
>   body?[225]

—so that divine justice has its foundation there, punishing in the children the fault of the fathers, in such a way that somehow paternal vices are imprinted in the souls of children, and that the disorder of the fathers' will touches them.

Further, some say that if souls came from anything except a natural series, and had been something else outside the body, they would have some clue to their first being, in addition to the natural faculties of discoursing, reasoning, and remembering:

> < . . . if the soul is placed in the body at birth,
> Why do we not remember the age already past
> Or hold any traces at all of things once done?>[226]

223. Virgil, Georgics, IV, 221–6.
224. Horace, Odes, IV, iv, 29.
225. Lucretius, De rerum natura, III, 741–5.
226. Lucretius, De rerum natura, III, 672–3.

For to give value to the condition of our souls as we wish to do, we would have to presuppose their omniscience when they are in their state of natural simplicity and purity. For when exempt from the prison of the body before they entered it as well as (according to our hope) after they had left it, they would have to have been like that. And when they were still in the body they would have to have some recollection of that knowledge, as Plato said that what we learn is only a recollection of what we once knew, something that everyone, on the basis of experience, can hold to be false. In the first place, insofar as we recall only what is taught us, and if memory has done its work properly, it would at least suggest to us something beyond the learning process. Secondly, if when it was pure, the soul possessed true knowledge, knowing things as they are through the divine intelligence, either there or here we make it accept lies and vices if we teach them to it! In this it cannot use its recollection since that image and conception had never been lodged in it. To say that the prison of the body stifles its naïve faculties in such a way that they are all extinguished: this is in the first place contrary to that other belief, that men can recognize such great forces and be aware of their operations in this life, forces so admirable that we have to infer from them that past divinity and eternity and the immortality to come:

> <For if the power of the mind is so much changed
> All remembrance of things past is lost to it,
> It is then, I believe, not very far from death.>[227]

Besides, it is here, in us and not elsewhere, that the powers and effects of the soul must be considered; all the rest of its perfections are vain and useless to it: it is for its present state that all its immortality must be paid and rewarded and from man's life alone that it is to be reckoned. It would be an injustice to deprive the soul of its means and its powers, to disarm it, in order to make a judgment and a condemnation of infinite and perpetual duration from the time of its captivity and its prison, from its weakness and malady, from the time when it had been forced and constrained—and to hold it to the consideration of so short a time, which may be of one or two hours or, at worst, a century, which has no more relation to the infinite than an instant, in order to regulate and establish definitely its whole being from that momentary interval. It would be an iniquitous disproportion to derive an eternal recompense from so short a life.

227. Lucretius, *De rerum natura*, III, 671–3.

<<Plato, in order to save himself from that difficulty, wants future payments to be limited to the duration of a hundred years relative to human duration, and our people have given them short enough temporal limits.>>

Thus they thought that the soul's generation followed the common condition of human things as did its life, according to the opinions of Epicurus and Democritus, which were the most generally accepted following those fair appearances: we see the soul born as soon as the body is capable of receiving it; we see it increase its powers as those of the body increase; the weakness of its infancy is manifest then, and, with time, so are its vigor and maturity; and then its decline, and its old age, and finally its decrepitude:

> . . . we feel that the mind is born with the body,
> And grows together with it, and with it comes to old age.[228]

They saw it capable of various passions and agitated by various painful movements, from which it fell into lassitude and pain, capable of alteration and of change, of joy, of drowsiness and languor, subject to its illnesses and its troubles, like the stomach and the foot:

> <We discern that the mind is healed while the body is sick,
> And we see it can be reestablished by medicine.>[229]

Dizzied and troubled by the power of wine, deprived of its stability by the vapors of a hot fever, put to sleep by the application of some medicines and awakened by others,

> <The mind must be bodily in nature,
> Since it suffers from the stroke of bodily weapons.>[230]

We see all its faculties astonished and reversed by the bite of a sick dog. In that condition it has no firmness of reasoning, no sufficiency, no virtue, no philosophical resolution, no contention of its forces great enough to be able to exempt it from subjection to these accidents. We see the saliva of a wretched cur, spilled on the hand of Socrates, shake all his wisdom and all his great and well-controlled ideas, destroying them, so that no trace remains of his prior consciousness:

228. Lucretius, De rerum natura, III, 445–6.
229. Lucretius, De rerum natura, III, 505–6.
230. Lucretius, De rerum natura, III, 176–7.

> *< . . . the force of the mind*
> *Is confounded, . . . and divided from itself*
> *It is tossed about, torn apart by that same poison.>*[231]

That poison finds no more resistance in this soul than in that of a four-year old child—poison capable of making all of philosophy, if it had been incarnate, furious and insane. Thus Cato, who defied even death and fortune, could not abide the sight of a mirror or of water, overcome by dread and terror when, from the bite of a mad dog, he had fallen into that illness that physicians call hydrophobia:

> *< . . . torn apart by the violence of disease,*
> *His soul is disturbed and foams, as in the salt sea*
> *The waves boil up from the fierce force of the wind.>*[232]

But as far as that is concerned, philosophy has armed man well against the suffering of all other accidents, either with patience, or if that costs too much to come by, with the infallible tactic of exempting himself entirely from feeling; but those are devices of use to a soul in possession of itself and with its wits about it, capable of discussion and deliberation, not to one in that disadvantageous state in which a philosopher's soul becomes that of a madman, disturbed, overturned and lost—a condition various circumstances produce as an overvehement agitation, which, through some strong passion, the soul can engender either in itself or as a wound in some part of the person or an exhalation of the stomach that throws us into vertigo or dizziness of the head;

> *< . . . in the diseases of the body, the mind often*
> *Wanders astray, for it loses its reason and speaks ravings;*
> *Sometimes in a heavy lethargy it is carried*
> *Into a deep and eternal sleep, with eyes and head*
> *nodding.>*[233]

It seems to me that the philosophers have not in the least touched this chord.

<<No more than they have another of equal importance. They always have this dilemma on their tongues to console us for our mortal condition: "Either the soul is mortal or it is immortal. If mortal, it will be

---

231. Lucretius, *De rerum natura*, III, 498–500.
232. Lucretius, *De rerum natura*, III, 494–6.
233. Lucretius, *De rerum natura*, III, 464–7.

without pain; if immortal, it will go on improving." They never touch the other horn of the dilemma: "What if it goes on getting worse?" and they leave to the poets the threats of future pains. But in that way they give themselves a good hand. There are two omissions that often occur to me in their arguments. I return to the first argument.>>

The deranged soul loses the taste of the Stoic sovereign good, so constant and so firm. Our fair wisdom must surrender and lay down its arms. Meanwhile, because of the vanity of human reason, the philosophers were led to consider that the mixture and association of two such different parts as the mortal and the immortal was unimaginable:

> For to link the mortal to the eternal and to think
> They can have the same feelings and act together
> Is folly. For what can be thought more contradictory
> And more discordant than that the mortal
> Should be linked in union with the immortal
> And everlasting to brave raging storms?[234]

What is more, they think the soul is involved in death, like the body:

> < . . . at the same time it grows weak with age>[235]

<<which, according to Zeno, the image of sleep shows us well enough; he thinks this a weakening and fall of the soul as well as of the body: "He thinks that the soul then contracts, that it is enfeebled and falls.">>[236] And the fact that some were seen to maintain their power and their vigor at the end of life, they attributed to the diversity of illnesses, as men in that extremity are perceived to maintain, some one sense, some another, some hearing, some smell, without alteration; and such universal weakening is not observed without some parts remaining complete and vigorous:

> <In the same way it may happen to some one
> That while his foot hurts, his head is in no pain.[237]

What our judgment has in view relates to truth as the brown owl's eye does to the splendor of the sun, as Aristotle says. How better could

234. Lucretius, *De rerum natura*, III, 801–6.
235. Lucretius, *De rerum natura*, III, 459.
236. Cicero, *De divinatione*, II, lviii.
237. Lucretius, *De rerum natura*, III, 113–4.

we convince ourselves than by such gross blindness in so obvious a
light?>

For the contrary opinion of the immortality of the soul, <<which
Cicero says was first introduced, at least according to the testimony of
the books, by Pherecydes Syrus at the time of King Tullus (some
attribute it to the invention of Thales, and some to others),>> this is the
part of human knowledge treated with the greatest reservation and
doubt. In this context the firmest dogmatists are chiefly constrained to
throw themselves under the protection of the shades of the Academy.
No one knows what Aristotle concluded on this subject, <<no more
than the ancients in general, who treat it with a vacillating belief: "*a
most agreeable thing, which they promise rather than prove.*">>[238] Aristotle conceals himself under the cloud of difficult and unintelligible
words and meanings, and has left his adherents to debate about his
judgment as much as about the subject matter itself. Two things make
that opinion plausible: one, that without the immortality of souls there
would be nothing on which to base the vain hopes of glory, which is a
consideration with wonderful standing in the world; the other, that it is
a very useful impression, <<as Plato says,>> that vices, when they escape
the obscure and uncertain sight of human justice, always remain
exposed to divine justice, which will pursue them even after the death
of the guilty.

<<An extreme concern makes man prolong his being; he has pro-
vided for this with respect to all his parts. For the conservation of the
body there are tombs; for the conservation of one's name, there is honor.

Impatient of his fate, he has used all his wits to build himself up and
to prop himself up by his inventions. Since the soul cannot stand on its
own feet due to its disturbance and its weakness, it goes looking everywhere for consolations, hopes, and foundations in the strange circumstances in which it finds itself and where it takes its place, and however
light and fanciful the things its ingenuity creates for it, the soul rests
there more securely and more willingly than in itself.>>

But it is remarkable that those most attached to this most just and
clear persuasion of the immortality of our minds have fallen short and
found themselves unable to establish it by their human powers: <<"*They
are the dreams of those who do not know, but choose,*">>[239] said an
ancient writer. On this evidence man can recognize that he owes to
luck and to circumstances the truth he alone discovers, since even

238. Seneca, *Epistles*, CII.
239. Cicero, *Academica*, II, xxxviii.

when it has fallen into his hand he has no way to seize it and keep it, and his reason does not have the power to take advantage of it. All things produced by our own reasoning and competence, the true as much as the false, are subject to uncertainty and debate. It is for the punishment of our pride and the instruction of our wretchedness and incapacity that God produced the difficulty and the confusion of the ancient tower of Babel. Everything we undertake without his help, everything we see except in the light of his grace, is only vanity and folly; the very essence of truth, which is uniform and constant, we corrupt and bastardize through our weakness when chance puts us in possession of it. Whatever course man undertakes on his own, God always allows him to arrive at the same confusion, by which he represents to us so vividly the image for the just punishment with which he strikes the presumptuousness of Nimrod and destroys the vain undertaking of the building of his pyramid: <<"*I shall confound the wisdom of the wise and reprove the prudence of the prudent.*">>[240] The diversity of idioms and of languages with which he disturbs that work: what is it but that infinite and perpetual altercation and discordance of opinions and arguments accompanying and confusing the vain construction of human knowledge? <<And confusing it usefully. Who would hold us back if we had a grain of knowledge? That saint gives me great pleasure: "*The concealment of what is useful is both an exercise in humility and a rein on pride.*"[241] To what point of presumption and of insolence do we not carry our blindness and our stupidity?>>

But to return to my subject, it was truly for good reason that we were held to God alone and to the favor of his grace for the truth of so noble a belief, since we receive from his bounty alone the fruit of immortality, which consists in the enjoyment of eternal blessedness.

<<Let us confess ingenuously that God alone has said this, together with faith: for it is not a lesson of nature and our reason. And anyone who will investigate his own being and his powers, both internal and external, without that divine gift, who will see man without flattering him, will see in him neither efficacy nor any faculty that smells of anything but death and earth. The more we give and owe and render to God, the more we act with greater Christianity.

What that Stoic philosopher says holds of the consent that happens to be given by the popular voice: should he not rather have held it from God? "*When we argue about the eternity of the soul, the consent of men*

240. 1 Corinthians 1:19.
241. Saint Augustine, *City of God*, XI, xxii.

who either fear or honor the infernal powers is of no small moment. I make use of this general conviction.">>[242]

But the weakness of human arguments on this subject is uniquely evident from the fabulous circumstances they have added as consequences of this opinion, in order to discover of what sort was this immortality of ours. <<Let us omit the Stoics who give souls a life after this, but a finite one: *They give us a long life, as they do crows; our souls will last a long time; but always, they deny.">>[243] The most universal and widely received opinion, which still survives in some places up to our own day, is the one attributed to Pythagoras, not that he is its first creator, but insofar as it receives great weight and credit from the authority of his approbation: that is that souls, in leaving us, do nothing but shift from one body to another, from a lion to a horse, from a horse to a king, traveling ceaselessly in this way from house to house.

<<And he himself said he remembered having been Aethalides, then Euphorbus, and afterward Hermotimus, and finally from Pyrrhus having passed to Pythagoras, so that he had a memory of himself for 206 years. Some philosophers added that these souls sometimes ascend to heaven and descend again:

> *Oh, father, is it to be thought that those lofty souls*
> *Go hence to heaven and again revert to heavy bodies?*
> *Why are those wretched ones so eager for the day?*[244]

Origen makes them go and come eternally from their good to their bad state. The view that Varro reports is that after 440 years of revolution they rejoin their first body; Chrysippus, that this can happen after a certain unlimited span of time.

Plato, who says that he takes from Pindar and from ancient poetry that belief in the infinite vicissitudes of change for which the soul is prepared, having in the other world no pains or rewards except temporal ones, since its life in this world is only temporal, infers that it has a unique knowledge of the affairs of heaven, of hell, and of this world through which it has passed, passed again, and dwelled during several voyages—a matter for its reminiscence.

This is the soul's further progress: he who has lived well joins the star to which he is assigned; he who has lived badly passes into a woman, and if he does not correct himself even then, he is changed into a beast

242. Seneca, *Epistles*, CXVII.
243. Cicero, *Tusculan Disputations*, I, xxxi.
244. Virgil, *Aeneid*, VI, 719–21.

of a sort suitable to his vicious habits, and he will not see the end of his punishments until he has returned to his native constitution, having rid himself through the power of reason of the gross, stupid, and elemental qualities that had been in him.>>

But I do not want to forget the objection that the Epicureans make to this transmigration from one body to another. It is amusing. They ask what order there would be if the press of the dying came to be greater than that of those being born, for the souls dislodged from their homes would be crowding to get first place in this new housing. And they also ask how those souls would pass the time while they were waiting for some lodging to be open for them. Or, on the contrary, if more animals were born than died, they say that the bodies would be in a parlous state, awaiting the infusion of their soul, and it would happen that some would die before being born:

Again, that souls should be present at couplings
And the birth of wild beasts seems ridiculous,
That immortal souls should stand waiting for mortal limbs
In innumerable numbers and struggle hastily with one
*   another*
As to which will be able to enter first.[245]

Others have kept the soul in the body of the departed so as to animate with it the snakes, worms, and other beasts that are said to be engendered from the corruption of our members, even of our ashes as well. Others divide the soul into one mortal part with the other part immortal. Other make it corporeal and yet at the same time immortal. Some make it immortal, without knowledge and without awareness. There are also those who have held that devils are made from the souls of the condemned <<(and some of our people have also believed that);>> Plutarch thinks that he can make gods of those that are saved, for there are few things that author has established with more conviction than in this case, maintaining everywhere else a doubtful and ambiguous manner. "It is necessary," he says, "to consider, and to believe firmly that, according to nature and divine justice, the souls of the virtuous are sainted by men and from being saints, become demigods, and that after they have been thoroughly cleansed and purified, as through sacrifices of purgation, and are freed of all susceptibility and of all mortality from being demigods, they become whole and perfect gods, not by any civil ordinance, but in truth and according to convincing argument, receiving a

245. Lucretius, *De rerum natura*, III, 776–81.

most happy and most glorious end."[246] But anyone who wants to see
him, who is among the most sober and moderate of the whole crowd, lay
about him with greater boldness and tell us miracles on this subject, I
refer to his treatises *On the Moon* and *Of the Daimon of Socrates*, where,
as clearly as anywhere else, he succeeds in persuading himself that the
mysteries of philosophy have many strange features in common with
those of poetry: human understanding losing itself by wanting to plumb
and examine all things to the bottom, just as, worn and exhausted by the
long course of our life, we return to childishness.—These are the fair
and certain lessons we draw from human knowledge on the subject of
our soul.

There is no less temerity in what philosophy teaches us about our
bodily parts. Let us choose one or two examples, for otherwise we
would lose ourselves in that vast and troubled sea of medical errors. Let
us decide if there is at least agreement on this: in what matter one man
produces another. <<For, as to their first production, it is no wonder if
human understanding is perplexed and distraught about something so
lofty and ancient. Archelaus the physician, whose disciple and favorite
Socrates was, according to Aristoxenus, said that both men and beasts
had been made from a milky slime put forth by the earth's heat.>>
Pythagoras said our seed is the foam of our finer blood; Plato, that it is
the distillation of the marrow of the backbone, which he infers from the
fact that this place is the first to feel fatigue and need; Alcmaeon, that it
is part of the substance of the brain, and that this is so, he says, is proved
by the fact that those who work too hard at that exercise have pains in
their eyes. Democritus says it is a substance extracted from the whole
mass of the body; Epicurus, extracted from the soul and the body; Aristotle, an excrement drawn from the food of the blood, the last that is dif-
fused through our limbs. Others say it is blood cooked and digested by
the heat of the genitals, which they judge to be so because in extreme
efforts men produce pure drops of blood—in this it seems there is more
likelihood, if any likelihood could be drawn from such infinite confusion. But, to bring this seed to do its work, how many contrary opinions
do they invent? Aristotle and Democritus hold that women have no
sperm and what they emit in the heat of pleasure and movement is only
a sweat that plays no part in generation. Galen and his followers, on the
contrary, hold that there can be no generation without the meeting of
seeds. Here are the physicians, the philosophers, the jurists, and the
theologians at odds, quarrelling with our wives on the dispute about the

246. Plutarch, *Lives*, XIV, "Life of Romulus."

term at which women bear fruit. And I, from my own example, join those among them who maintain a pregnancy of eleven months.[247] The world is built on this experience, and yet there is no little woman so simple that she cannot give her opinion in all these debates, and still we cannot agree.

That is enough to confirm that man is no better instructed in the knowledge of himself in the physical than in the spiritual part. We have proposed himself to himself and his reason to his reason to see what it could tell us. It seems to me that we have shown sufficiently how little reason understands of itself.

<<And he who does not understand himself, what can he understand?

"As if he could understand the measure of any other thing, who does not know his own."[248]

Truly, Protagoras was telling a fine tale when he made man the measure of all things, although man never knew his own measure. If man were not himself the standard, his dignity would not allow any other creature to have that advantage. But as for man himself, since he was so contrary in himself, one judgment constantly overturning another, this favorable proposition was only a joke, which necessarily led us to infer the nothingness of the measure and the measurer.

When Thales considers the knowledge of man very difficult for man, he teaches him at the same time that all other knowledge is impossible for him.>>

You,[249] for whom I have taken the trouble of stretching out so long a body of writing, contrary to my custom, do not refuse to support your Sebond by the ordinary form of argument, in which you are instructed every day and in which you will exercise your wit and your learning, for this last fencing trick is never to be employed except as an extreme remedy. It is a desperate thrust, in which you must abandon your arms in order to make your opponent lose his, and a secret turn that must be used rarely and with reservation. It is great temerity for you to destroy yourself in order to destroy another.

247. Physicians generally accepted as legitimate children who were born in a pregnancy lasting eleven months (cf. Rabelais, *Gargantua*, III), as allegedly happened in Montaigne's case.

248. Pliny, *Naturalis historia*, II, 1.

249. Montaigne is addressing Marguerite de Valois (1553–1615), daughter of Henry II and Catherine de Medici, who in 1572 married Henry, a Protestant and the king of Navarre, later Henry IV of France; the marriage was annulled in 1599.

<You must not wish to die to avenge yourself, as Gobrias did—for when he was grappling closely in combat with a Persian lord, and Darius, approaching with sword in hand, feared to strike lest he should hit Gobrias, the latter shouted at him that he should strike boldly, even though he would have to run them both through at once.>

<<I have seen rejected when they were offered arms and conditions of combat so desperate that it is beyond belief that either the one or the other could survive. In the Indian ocean the Portuguese took fourteen Turks who, impatient of their captivity, resolved—and they succeeded—to reduce both themselves and their masters, and the vessel itself, to ashes, rubbing the nails of the ship against one another, so that a spark of fire fell on the barrels of gunpowder that were there.>>

Here we reach the limits and outer bounds of the sciences, whose extremity is vicious, as is the case with virtue. Hold yourself on the common road; it is no good at all to be so subtle and so fine. Remember what the Tuscan proverb says: "*If you spread yourself too thin, you'll break.*"[250] In your opinions and in your discourse as well as in your customs and in everything else, I recommend to you moderation and temperance and the avoidance of novelty and eccentricity. All extravagant ways make me angry. You who, by the authority your greatness gives you, and still more by the advantages provided by your own unique qualities, can command whomever you like at the blink of an eye, ought to have given this charge to someone who made a profession of letters, who could much better have supported and enriched this idea. However, here is as much of it as you will need.

Epicurus said of the laws that the worst were so necessary that without them men would eat one another. <<And Plato, in almost the same way, said that without laws we would live like brute beasts, and he tries to verify this.>> Our mind is a wandering, dangerous, and foolhardy utensil; it is difficult to join to it any order and measure. And in my time, those who have that rare excellence beyond others, and some extraordinary vivacity—we see them almost all dissipated in the licentiousness of their opinions and their habits. It is a miracle if we find one who is moderate and sociable. It is right to give the human mind the narrowest possible barriers. In study, as in everything else, we must count and regulate its steps; we must cut down by art the limits of its inquiry. It is bridled and pinioned by religions, laws, customs, knowledge, precepts, mortal and immortal punishments and rewards; yet we see that by its volubility and dissolution, it escapes all those

250. Petrarch, *Canzoniere*, XXII, 48.

bonds. It is a vain body, with nothing by which it can be seized or struck, a diverse and deformed body we can neither tie up nor grasp. <Surely there are few souls so controlled, so strong, and so well-born as to be able to be trusted with their own conduct and who can, with moderation and without temerity, advance in the freedom of their judgments beyond common opinions. It is more expedient to place souls under instruction.

Mind is a dangerous sword, <<even to its possessor,>> if he does not know how to fortify himself with it regularly and discreetly.> <<And there is not a beast to whom blinkers are more properly given to keep his sight governed and limited before his feet and to keep him from wandering here and there, beyond the tracks that custom and the laws lay out for him.>> That is why it will be better for you to confine yourself within the accustomed path, whatever it is, than to fly off with that unbridled liberty. But if one of those new doctors tries to exhibit his ingenuity in your presence, at the risk of his salvation and of yours, to save you from that dangerous pestilence, which spreads every day on your path, in extreme necessity this preservative will prevent the contagion of that poison from harming either you or those around you.

[6. Man's Claims to Knowledge Are Defective]

But the freedom and gaiety of those ancient minds produced in philosophy and the human sciences several sects of different opinions, each one undertaking to judge and to choose what side to take. But now <<that all men take one path, men *"who are confined and committed to certain fixed and determinate opinions to the point where they are reduced to defending even things of which they do not approve,"*[251] and>> now that we receive the arts by civil authority and ordinance, <<so that the schools have only one model and a like constitution and discipline,>> we no longer consider what coins weigh and are worth, but everyone in his turn receives them at the price that common approbation and circulation gives them. No case is made for the alloy, but for its usage: in this way all things are made equal. Medicine is received like geometry, and the mountebank's tricks, enchantments, infatuations, communication with the spirits of the dead, prognostications, domifications, and even that ridiculous pursuit of the philosopher's stone all this goes on without contradiction. We need to know no more than that the seat of Mars is lodged in the middle of the triangle of the hand, that of Venus in the thumb, and of Mercury in the lit-

251. Cicero, *Tusculan Disputations*, II, ii.

tle finger, and that when the heart line cuts the tubercle of the forefinger, that is a sign of cruelty; that when it falls short of the middle finger and the natural median line makes an angle with the vital in the same place, that is the sign of a miserable death; and that if, in a woman, the natural line is open and does not make an angle with the vital, this means that she will be questionably chaste. I call you yourself to witness whether a man with that knowledge cannot pass with reputation and favor in all companies.

Theophrastus said that human knowledge acquired through the senses could judge the causes of things to a certain degree, but that when it came to the ultimate first causes, it had to stop and retire, either because of its own weakness or because of the difficulty of things. This is a moderate and gentle opinion, that our sufficiency can lead us to the knowledge of some things, and that it has certain degrees of power beyond which it is temerity to use it. This opinion is plausible and is introduced by men of well-ordered minds; but it is hard to give boundaries to our mind, because it is curious and greedy and has no more reason to stop at a thousand paces than at fifty. We have found by experience that where one has failed, another has succeeded; that what was unknown in one century has been explained in the next; that the sciences and arts are not cast in a mold, but are formed and fashioned little by little, reworked and polished several times, just as bears gradually lick their cubs into shape. In the same way I do not stop sounding and attempting what my power cannot discover, handling and kneading this new matter over and over, turning it over and heating it. Thus I open to my successor some facility for enjoying it at his ease and make it suppler and more manageable for him,

> . . . as the wax of Hymettus, softened in the sun,
> When pressed by the thumb takes many shapes,
> And becomes fit for this very task.[252]

The second person will do as much for the third, which is why the difficulty should not make me despair, no more than my impotence, since it is only mine. Man is as capable of all things as of some, and if, as Theophrastus says, he confesses ignorance of first causes and of principles, let him at once give up all the rest of his knowledge; if he lacks the foundation, his reason is overthrown. Dispute and inquiry have no other end and stopping place but principles; if that end does not stop his course, he is throwing himself into an infinite irresolution. <<"One

252. Ovid, Metamorphoses, X, 284–6.

*thing cannot be comprehended more or less than another, since the defi-
nition of comprehension of all things is one."*>>[253]
   But it is probable that if the soul knew anything it would first know
itself, and if it knew anything outside itself, that would be its own body
and its casing before anything else. If today we still see the gods of medicine debating about our anatomy—

   Vulcan stood against Troy, Apollo for Troy[254]

—when do we expect them to agree? We are closer to ourselves than
whiteness is to snow or weight to stone. If man does not know himself,
how can he know his functions and his powers? It is not that we do not
happen to have in us some real knowledge, but it is there by chance.
For since errors are received into our soul by the same path, the same
fashion, and the same process, there is no way to distinguish them, or
any way to choose truth rather than falsehood.
   The Academics admitted a certain tendency of judgment, and found
it too crude to say that it was in no way more probable that snow was
white than black, and that we could be no more certain of the movement of a stone thrown by our hand than of the movement of the
eighth sphere. And to avoid this difficulty and strangeness, which can in
truth live only awkwardly in our imagination, although they established
that we are never in any way capable of knowledge and that truth is
lodged in deep chasms which human sight cannot penetrate, still they
considered some things more probable than others, and admitted into
their judgment this faculty of being able to incline rather to one appearance than to another; they allowed their judgment this propensity,
while denying it all resolution.
   The opinion of the Pyrrhonians is bolder and somewhat more
likely. For what is that Academic inclination and propensity toward
one proposition rather than another but the recognition of some truth
more apparent in this than in that? If our understanding were capable
of the form, the lineaments, the bearing, and the face of truth, it would
see the truth whole rather than by halves, just coming into being, and
imperfect. Increase this appearance of verisimilitude that makes them
lean rather to the left than the right; multiply that ounce of verisimilitude that inclines the balance a hundred, a thousand times, it will
finally come about that the balance will take one side entirely, and will
stop at a choice and a complete truth. But why do they let themselves

253. Cicero, *Academica*, II, xli.
254. Ovid, *Tristia*, I, ii, 5.

be swayed by verisimilitude if they do not know the truth? How do they recognize the semblance of something whose essence they do not know? How can we judge in fact where in fact we cannot? If our intellectual and sensible faculties are without foundation and without footing, if they only float and blow about, it is for nothing that we let our judgment be carried off to any part of their operation, whatever appearance it may present to us; and the most secure seat for our understanding, and the happiest, would be where it would keep itself calm, erect, inflexible, without motion, and without agitation. <<"*Among appearances, whether true or false, there is no difference for the assent of the mind.*">>[255]

We see well enough that things are not lodged in us in their form and essence and do not make their entrance on their own power and authority, from the fact that if this were so we would receive them in the same way: wine would be the same in the mouth of the sick man as in that of the healthy one. A person who had chapped or numbed fingers would find in the wood or the iron that he handles the same hardness that anyone else does. But alien subjects submit to our whim; they lodge in us as we please. Now if on our part we received anything without alteration, if human grasp were capable and solid enough to seize the truth by our own means, these means being common to all men, that truth would be passed from hand to hand, from one to the other. And of as many things as there are in the world, at least one would be found that would be accepted by all men with universal consent. But the fact that there is no one proposition that is not or cannot be open to debate and controversy among us shows plainly that our natural judgment does not grasp very clearly what it grasps, for my judgment cannot get itself accepted in the judgment of my companion, which is a sign that I have grasped it by some means other than by a natural power in me and in all men.

Let us leave aside that infinite confusion of opinions apparent among the philosophers themselves, and that perpetual and universal debate about the knowledge of things. For this is truly presupposed, that men—I mean the learned, the best born, the most competent—do not agree on anything, not even that the sky is above our heads, for those who doubt everything doubt that, too, and those who deny that we can understand anything say that we have not understood that the sky is above our heads; and these two opinions are incomparably the greatest in number.

255. Cicero, *Academica*, II, xxviii.

Besides this infinite diversity and division it is easy to see from the trouble our judgment gives us and from the uncertainty everyone feels in himself that the seat of judgment is very insecure. How diversely do we judge of things? How many times do we change our ideas? What I hold and what I believe today, I hold and believe with my whole belief; all my instruments and resources seize and take hold of this opinion, and are responsible to me for it, as much as in them lies. I would not know how to embrace any truth or maintain it with more force than I do that one. I am with it entirely and absolutely; but has it not happened to me, not once, but a hundred, but a thousand times, but every day, that I have embraced with all the same implements and in the same condition some other thing that I have since judged to be false? At least we have to grow wise at our own expense. If I often find myself betrayed by a particular color, if my touch usually proves false and my balance unequal and inexact, what assurance can I have this time more than others? Is it not stupidity to let myself be so often duped by the same guide? Still, let fortune move us about five hundred times, let her treat our belief like a vessel to be emptied and filled with constantly changing opinions, the present and the latest one is always certain and infallible. For it we have to abandon goods, honor, life, health, and everything:

> . . . the thing found later
> Destroys and changes all our feelings for the old things.[256]

<Whatever is preached to us, whatever we learn, it must always be remembered that it is man who gives and man who receives; it is a mortal hand that presents it to us, it is a mortal hand that receives it. Only the things that come to us from heaven have the right and authority to persuade; only they have the mark of truth. Nor do we see that mark with our eyes or receive it by our means: that holy and great image would not be received in so wretched a dwelling if God did not prepare it for this purpose, if God did not reform and fortify it by his great and particular and supernatural favor.>

At least our faulty condition should make us behave more moderately and with more reservation in our changes. We should remember that, whatever we receive in our understanding, we often receive falsehoods there, and by these same instruments, which often give themselves the lie and are deceived.

256. Lucretius, *De rerum natura*, V, 1413–4.

Now it is no wonder that they give themselves the lie, since they are so easily turned and swayed by very slight occurrences. It is certain that our apprehension, our judgment, and the faculties of our soul in general suffer according to the movements and alterations of the body, alterations that are continual. Do we not have our minds more awakened, our memories quicker, our discourse more lively in health than in sickness? Do not joy and gaiety make us receive the subjects presented to our souls with quite a different face than do chagrin and melancholy? Do you think the verses of Catullus or of Sappho smile at an avaricious, doting old man as they do at a vigorous and ardent youth? <When Cleomenes, son of Anaxandridas, was ill, his friends reproached him for new and unaccustomed humors and ideas. "You are right," he said, "nor am I the same person I was when I was well; since I am different, so are my opinions and fancies."> In the disputes of our law courts this expression is in common use, spoken of criminals who encounter judges in a good humor, gentle and mild: "Let him rejoice in his good luck;" for it is certain that judgments are sometimes more inclined to condemnation, thornier, and harsher, at other times laxer, easier, and more inclined to pardon. A man who brings from his house the pain of gout, jealousy, or theft by his valet, since he has his soul colored and drenched with anger, will doubtless have his judgment changed in that direction. <That venerable senate of the Areopagus used to make its judgments at night for fear that the appearance of the parties might corrupt its judgment.> The very air and serenity of the heavens produce some change in us, as this Greek verse in Cicero attests:

> The minds of men resemble the way
> Father Jupiter himself lights the fruitful earth with his
>   torch.[257]

It is not only fevers, debauches, and great accidents that overturn our judgment; the least things in the world upset it. And there can be no doubt, even if we are not aware of it, that if a continuous fever can overwhelm the soul, the tertian fever can produce some change according to its degree and proportion. If apoplexy stupefies and extinguishes entirely our mental vision, there can be no doubt that a heavy chill will make it dizzy. And consequently a single hour can scarcely be found in life in which our judgment takes its proper place—our body being subject to such constant changes and stuffed with so many kinds of mecha-

257. Homer, *Odyssey* (trans. Cicero); cited by Saint Augustine, *City of God*, VIII.

nisms that (as I believe on the word of the physicians) some one of them is always likely to be out of order.

For the rest, this illness does not show itself so easily unless it is quite extreme and irremediable, insofar as reason always hobbles, limps, and goes askew with falsehood as with truth. Thus it is hard to discover when it is mistaken and disordered. I always call reason that appearance of rationality everyone forges in himself, that reason which can be in such a state that there are a hundred contraries on the same subject is an instrument of lead and wax, ductile, pliable, and able to accommodate itself to every bias and to every standard. Nothing remains but the skill to know how to mold it. However good a judge's intentions, if he does not take care, as few like to do, the partiality to friendship, to kinship, to beauty and to vengeance—and not only such weighty things, but that chance instinct that makes us favor one thing rather than another, and, without reason's permission, gives us a choice between two equal subjects or some equally slight shadow—these can insinuate insensibly into our judgment the approval or disapproval of some cause and tilt the balance.

I, who am watching over myself as closely as possible, who have my eyes incessantly turned on myself, like someone who has nothing much to do elsewhere,

> . . . *who does not care*
> *What king is feared in the cold region under the Arctus,*
> *Or who terrifies Tyridates,*[258]

I shall hardly dare to report the emptiness and weakness I find in myself. My footing is so unstable and unsteady; I find it so easy to totter and am so ready to reel, and my sight is so disordered that when fasting I feel myself quite different from what I am after a meal. If my health and a fair day smile on me, here I am, an agreeable fellow; if I have a corn pressing on my toe, here I am: sullen, out of humor, and inaccessible. <The same pace of a horse now seems to me difficult, now easy, and the same path seems at this hour shorter, another time longer, and the same shape now more, now less agreeable.> Now I want to do everything, now nothing; what is a pleasure to me at this time will sometimes be a pain. A thousand indiscreet and casual agitations occur in me. Either the melancholy or the choleric humor has hold of me; at this hour, by its own special authority, sadness dominates in me, and at that hour, cheerfulness. When I pick up books, I will have found in such

258. Horace, *Odes*, I, xxvi, 3–6.

and such passages excellent graces that would have touched my soul; if I happen on them at some other time, it is no use tossing and turning them, it is no use folding and handling them, it is an unknown and shapeless mass for me.

<Even in my own writings I do not always find the feeling of what I had first imagined; I do not know what I wanted to say, and I am often provoked into making corrections and even inserting a new sense because I have lost the earlier one, which was better. I just go back and forth: my judgment does not always advance; it floats, it wanders,

> *. . . like a small boat*
> *Tossed in the sea by a furious wind.*[259]

Often when, as I am inclined to do on purpose, I have taken it up as an exercise and a game to maintain an opinion contrary to my own, my mind, turning and applying itself that way, attaches itself so well to the contrary opinion that I no longer find any reason for my earlier view, and abandon it. I am led astray, as it were, by the side I am leaning toward, whatever it is, and carried off by my own weight.

Almost everyone could say as much of himself, if he looked at himself as I do. Preachers know that emotion comes to them when they are speaking and moves them toward belief, and that in anger we devote ourselves more thoroughly to the defense of our proposition, imprint it in ourselves, and embrace it with more vehemence and approbation than we do when we are in our cold and quiet state. You simply report a case to your lawyer; he replies to you unsteadily and doubtfully: you feel that it is indifferent to him to begin supporting one or the other side; if you have paid him well to chew on it and to get excited about it, does he begin to be interested, has his will warmed up? His reason and knowledge are heated to a certain degree; here is an apparent and indubitable truth that presents itself to his understanding; he discovers a wholly new light there, believes it in all earnest, and persuades himself accordingly. Indeed, I do not know whether the ardor that springs from spite and obstinacy when one is faced with the pressure and violence of the magistrate and danger, <<or the interest of reputation,>> <has not led some men to maintain, even to the stake, the opinion for which, among friends and at liberty, they would not have burned a fingertip.>

The shakings and agitations our soul receives from bodily passions can do much in it, but more can be done by its own proper passions, to which it is so fully subject that it could perhaps be claimed it has no

259. Catullus, *Poems*, XXV, 12–3.

other pace or movement but from the breath of those winds, and without their agitation it would remain without action, like a ship in the open sea deprived of the winds' assistance. And anyone who, <<siding with the Peripatetics,>> would maintain this, would not do us much wrong, since it is known that most of the soul's finest actions proceed from and need that impulsion of the passions. Courage, they say, cannot be perfect without the assistance of anger:

<<*Ajax, always brave, is bravest when angry.*[260]

Nor do we rush vigorously enough at the wicked and at our enemies if we are not angry. And we want the lawyer to inspire anger in the judge in order to obtain justice. Irregular desires move Themistocles, move Demosthenes, and have pushed the philosophers to labors, vigils, and peregrinations; they lead us to honor, learning, health: all useful ends. And this fear of the soul to suffer boredom and anger serves to nourish penitence and remorse in the conscience and to make us feel as our punishment the scourge of God and the scourge of the state's correction.>> Compassion serves as a spur to <clemency, and the prudence to conserve and govern ourselves is awakened by our fear; and how many fine actions by ambition? How many by presumption?> In short, no brave and vigorous virtue is without some disordered agitation. Would that be one of the reasons that moved the Epicureans to discharge God of all care and solicitude for our affairs, insofar as the very effects of his goodness could not be exercised toward us without shattering our repose by means of the passions, which are like spurs and attractions guiding the soul to virtuous actions? <<Or did they perhaps think otherwise, and take them for storms that shamefully entice the soul from its tranquillity? *"As the sea is thought to be tranquil when not even the slightest breath of air is stirring, so the soul's state is seen to be quiet and at peace when no perturbation can move it."*>>[261]

What differences of sense and reason, what contrariety of imaginings the diversity of our passions presents to us! So what assurance can we have of something so unstable and so mobile, subject by its condition to the dominance of trouble <<and then going only at a forced and borrowed pace?>> If our judgment is in the hands of sickness itself and perturbation, if it is from madness and temerity that it is confined to receiving the impressions of things, what certainty can we expect from it?

260. Cicero, *Tusculan Disputations*, IV, xxiii.
261. Cicero, *Tusculan Disputations*, V, v.

<<Is it not bold of philosophy to consider that men produce their greatest deeds and those most approaching divinity when they are beside themselves and furious and mad? We improve ourselves by the privation of our reason and its slumber. The two natural ways to enter into the cabinet of the gods and to foresee the course of destiny are madness and sleep. This is pleasant to consider: by the dislocation that the passions bring to our reason we become virtuous; by the extirpation that madness or the image of death bring to it we become prophets and seers. Never was I more willing to believe anything. It is pure enthusiasm that sacred truth has breathed into the philosophic mind, which extracts from it, against its own proposition, the thesis that the tranquil state of our soul, the composed state, the most healthful state that philosophy can gain for it is not its best state. Our waking state is more asleep than sleep itself; our wisdom, less wise than folly; our dreams are worth more than our reasonings. The worst place we could occupy is in ourselves. But does not philosophy think we are clever enough to notice that the voice that makes mind, when disjoined from man, so far-seeing, so great, so perfect, and while it is in man so earthbound, ignorant, and dark, is a voice proceeding from the mind that is part of earthbound man, ignorant and dark, and for that reason a voice not to be trusted or believed?>>

Being of a soft and heavy complexion, I have no great experience of those vehement agitations, most of which suddenly surprise our soul without giving it leisure to recognize itself. But that passion said to be produced by idleness in the hearts of young men, although it proceeds in a leisurely way and with a measured progress, quite plainly demonstrates, to those who have tried to oppose its power, the force of that conversion and alteration our judgment suffers. I formerly tried to keep myself taut to resist and repel it—for I am so far from being one of those who seek vices, that I follow them only when they drag me along. I felt it arise, grow, and increase despite my resistance, and finally, all-seeing and vivid, seize and possess me in such a way that the images of things began to seem to me other than they used to, as in drunkenness. I saw clearly increasing and growing the advantages of the object I was desirous of, and expanding through the influence of my imagination, the difficulties of my enterprise easing and smoothing themselves out, my reason and my conscience withdrawing. But when this fire was extinguished, all of a sudden, as with a flash of lightning, I saw my soul take another sort of view, another state, and another judgment. I saw the difficulties of retreat appear great and invincible and the same things with an entirely different taste and appearance than the heat of desire had presented them as having. Which was more probable? Pyrrho has no idea. We are never without illness. Fevers have their hot and their cold spells; from the effects of a burning passion we revert to the effects of a shivering one.

<As much as I had thrown myself ahead, so much do I fall back:

> *Thus it is that the sea, changing its tides,*
> *Sometimes foams up earth on the rocks*
> *And spreads itself far on the sandy shore,*
> *Sometimes, in receding, takes back its pebbles*
> *And leaves the shore bare with an ebbing flow.>*[262]

Now from the knowledge of my mutability I have brought about in myself some constancy of opinions, and I have not at all altered those I had first and naturally. For whatever appearance of truth there may be in novelty, I do not change easily for fear of losing by the change. And when I am not capable of choosing, I take someone else's choice and hold myself in the place where God has put me. Otherwise I would not know how to keep myself from rolling endlessly. Thus by the grace of God I have preserved entirely, without agitation and trouble of conscience, the ancient beliefs of our religion through all the sects and divisions our century has produced. The writings of the ancients—I mean the good writings, full and solid—hold me and move me more or less as they wish; the person I hear always seems to me the strictest; I find each one right in his turn, although they contradict one another. This facility that good minds have for making what they like sound probable, and the fact that there is nothing so strange that they cannot undertake to give it enough color to deceive a simplicity like mine: this shows clearly the weakness of their demonstration. The sky and the stars have been moving for three thousand years; everyone believed that until <<Cleanthes the Samian or, according to Theophrastus, Nicetas of Syracuse>> decided to assert it was the earth that was moving, <<rotating on its axis through the oblique circle of the Zodiac,>> and in our day Copernicus has established that doctrine so well that it is regularly used for all astronomical inferences. What can we learn from this except that it should not matter to us which of the two is true? And who knows if, a thousand years from now, a third opinion will not overturn the two preceding ones?

> *So rolling time changes the fate of things;*
> *What was of value becomes of no worth;*
> *And then something else rises and leaves its place of scorn,*

262. Virgil, *Aeneid*, 624–8.

Is desired more and more each day,
When found, blossoms with praise
And is of wondrous honor among mortals.[263]

Thus when any new doctrine is presented to us, we have great reason to distrust it and to consider that before it was produced, its contrary was in vogue; and that, as the earlier one was overturned by this one, in the future a third invention will arise that will in turn strike down the second. Before the principles Aristotle introduced were esteemed, other principles satisfied human reason as the former satisfy us at this hour. What patent have they, what special privilege do they have, so that the course of our invention stops with them and that their hold on our belief should continue for all time to come? They are no more exempt from being turned out of doors than were their predecessors. When I am urged to accept a new argument, it is up to me to decide that what I cannot answer, another may. For to believe all likelihoods we cannot disprove would be very simple-minded. From this it would follow that all the vulgar—<<and we are all among the vulgar>>—would have their belief as easy to turn as a weathervane. For our soul, being soft and without resistance, would be forced to receive ceaselessly other and still other impressions, the last one always effacing the trace of the former. Whoever feels himself weak should reply, following practice, that he will speak of it to his adviser or will report it to the wiser people from whom he received his instruction. How long has medicine been in the world? They say that a newcomer, called Paracelsus, is changing and reversing the whole order of the ancient rules, and maintains that up to this time the old order has only served to make men die. I believe he will easily verify that, but I do not find it would be very wise to put my life to the test of his new experience.

We are not to believe everyone, says the precept, since anyone can say anything.

A man of that profession of novelties and reforms in physics told me not long ago that all the ancients had obviously mistaken the nature and movements of the winds, which he said he would make quite palpable if I would listen to him. After I had patiently heard his arguments, which looked extremely probable, I asked him: "How did those who navigated according to the laws of Theophrastus go west when they were headed east? Did they go sideways or backwards?" "That's as may be," he replied to me, "but they were mistaken." I then answered that I preferred to follow facts than reason.

263. Lucretius, *De rerum natura*, V, 1275–9.

Now these things often contradict one another, and I have been told that in geometry (which claims to have gained the highest point of certainty in the sciences) there are necessary demonstrations that subvert the truth of experience: as Jacques Peletier was telling me at my house, he had found two lines approaching one another so as to meet, which he showed could nevertheless not succeed in touching one another, even at infinity. The Pyrrhonians use their arguments and reason only to destroy the apparent facts of experience, and it is remarkable how far the suppleness of our reason has followed their plan of opposing the evidence of facts: for they confirm that we cannot move, that we cannot speak, that there is nothing heavy or hot, with the same kind of forceful arguments by which we confirm more probable facts. Ptolemy, who was a great figure, had established the limits of our world; all the ancient philosophers thought they knew its measure, except for certain remote islands that might escape their knowledge. It was Pyrrhonizing, a thousand years ago, to place in doubt the science of cosmography and the opinions that had been received from each of them. <It was heresy to admit the antipodes.> Now in our century there is an infinite stretch of *terra firma* that has been discovered, not an island or a particular country, but a part almost equal in size to what we used to know. The geographers of our time do not hesitate to assure us that now everything has been discovered and everything is seen:

For what is at hand pleases us and is seen to excel.[264]

Since Ptolemy was formerly mistaken on the foundations of his argument, how should I know if it would not be folly on my part now to trust what they say about it, <<and if it is not more likely that this huge body we call the world is something else than what we now believe?

Plato says that it changes countenance in every way, that the sky, the stars, and the sun sometimes reverse the movement we see there, changing the east to the west. The Egyptian priests told Herodotus that since their first king, eleven thousand years or so ago (and they showed him the effigies of all their kings in statues taken from the life), the sun had changed its course four times; that the sea and the earth change alternately into one another; that the birth of the world is indeterminate. Aristotle and Cicero say the same. And someone among us says that from all eternity the world is mortal and is reborn in various vicissitudes, calling to witness Solomon and Isaiah, to avoid those objections that God has sometimes been a creator without a creature, that he was

264. Lucretius, *De rerum natura*, V, 1411.

idle, that he got rid of his idleness by putting his hand to this work, and that consequently he is subject to change. In the most famous of the Greek schools the world is considered a god made by another greater god, and is composed of a body and a soul lodged at its center and expanding by musical numbers to its circumference, divine, most happy, most great, most wise, eternal. In it are other gods, the earth, the sea, the stars, which support one another with an harmonious and perpetual agitation and divine dance, sometimes encountering one another, sometimes retreating, hiding themselves, showing themselves, changing their order, now in front and now behind. Heraclitus established that the world was made of fire and, by the order of destinies, must one day be enflamed and consumed by fire and one day again renewed. And men, said Apuleius, are *"mortal in particular, but immortal in general."*[265] Alexander wrote to his mother the story told by an Egyptian priest, derived from their monuments, testifying to the infinite age of that nation and including the birth and progress of other countries. Cicero and Diodorus say of their time that the Chaldeans kept a record of some four hundred thousand years. Aristotle, Pliny, and others say that Zoroaster lived six thousand years before the age of Plato. Plato says that those of the city of Sais have memoirs in writing of eight thousand years, and that the city of Athens was built a thousand years before that of Sais. <Epicurus says that at the same time things are as we now see them, they are entirely similar, and in the same way, in a number of other worlds. That is what he would have said more confidently if he had seen the similarities and agreements, in so many strange examples present and past, of that new world of the West Indies with ours.>

In truth, considering what has come to our knowledge of the course of that terrestrial order, I am often surprised to see, at so great a distance of place and time, the concurrence of a great number of monstrous popular opinions and savage beliefs, which seem by no means to proceed from our natural reasoning. The human mind is a great worker of miracles; but this relation has in it something, I know not what, that is more extraordinary—it is found also in names, in accidents, and in a thousand other things. <For nations have been found there having, so far as we know, no news of us, where circumcision was approved; where there were states and great civil governments maintained only by women, without men; where our fasts and Lent were represented, combined with abstinence from women; where our crosses were in use in different ways: here sepulchers were honored with them; there they were used,

265. Apuleius, cited by Saint Augustine, *City of God*, XII, x.

and in particular that of Saint Andrew, to protect oneself against noctur-
nal visions and were set on the beds of children against magic spells.
Elsewhere they encountered one of them made of wood, of great
height, adored as god of the rain—and this a long way in the interior.
There was found an entirely exact likeness of our penitential priests, the
use of miters, the celibacy of the clergy, the art of divination through the
entrails of sacrificed animals,> abstinence from all sorts of flesh and fish
in their diet; the habit of priests of using a special language, and not the
vulgar tongue; and that fanciful idea, that the first god was driven out by
a second, his younger brother; that they were created with all sorts of
conveniences that had been taken from them for their sins, their territory changed and their natural condition worsened; that of old they had
been submerged by the inundation of the waters of heaven; that only a
few families were saved, who fled into the high mountain caves, which
they stopped up so that the water could not get into them, when they
had shut in their various kinds of animals; that when they thought the
rain was stopping, they sent out dogs, who came back clean and wet, so
that they thought the water had not yet receded far enough; afterward,
when they sent out others and saw them come back dirty, they went out
to re-people the world, which they found full only of snakes.

Belief in the judgment day was found in one place, so that the people there were extremely angry at the Spaniards, who spread the bones
of the deceased when rifling the treasures of sepulchers, saying that
these scattered bones could not easily be rejoined; trade by exchange
and no other way, fairs and markets for this purpose; dwarves and
deformed persons to adorn the banquets of princes; the use of falconry,
following the nature of their birds; tyrannical subsidies; refinements in
gardening; dances, tumbling tricks, instrumental music; coats of arms;
tennis courts, games of dice and chance, in which they sometimes
become so heated that they risk themselves and their freedom; medicine only by charms; the method of writing in figures; belief in a single
first man, father of all the peoples; adoration of a god who once lived as
a man in perfect virginity, fasting, and penitence, preaching the law of
nature and the ceremonies of religion and who disappeared from the
world without a natural death; the belief in giants; the habit of becoming drunk from their beverages and of drinking as much as possible;
religious ornaments painted with the bones and skulls of the dead; sur-
plices; holy water, sprinkled; women and servants who present themselves freely to be burned and buried with the deceased husband or
master; the law that the eldest inherits everything, and no part is
reserved for the younger except obedience; the custom according to
which at promotion to a certain office of high authority, the one who is

promoted takes a new name and gives up the name he had; strewing lime on the knee of a newborn child, saying to him: "Dust you are, and to dust you shall return"; the art of augury.

These empty shadows of our religion that are seen in some examples testify to its dignity and divinity. It has insinuated itself by a certain imitation not only into all the infidel nations on this side of the world, but also into those barbarians by a common and supernatural inspiration. For we find there also the belief in purgatory, but in a new form; what we give to fire they give to cold, and imagine souls purged and punished by the rigor of an extreme chill. And this example reminds me of another amusing difference: for as there are some peoples who love to uncover the end of their member, in the manner of the Mohammedans or the Jews, there are others who were so concerned about making it bare that they carefully stretch their skin over the end and attach it with little strings above, for fear that the end would reach the air. And there is this difference also: that as we honor kings and festivals by wearing the best clothes we have, in some regions, to show their disparity and submission to their king, the subjects present themselves to him in their worst clothing and when they enter his palace put some old torn robe over their good one, in order that the luster and ornament be all the master's. But let us continue.>>

If, as it does all other things, nature encloses in the bounds of its progress the beliefs, judgments, and opinions of men; if they have their revolution, their rationale, their birth, their death, as cabbages do; if the heaven agitates and moves them about at its pleasure, what magisterial and permanent authority do we attribute to them? <If we see by experience that the form of our being depends on the air, the climate, and the territory where we are born, not only the color, the stature, the complexion, and the countenances, but even the faculties of the soul>—<<"*The climate affects the vigor not only of bodies, but of minds as well*," says Vegetius[266]—and that the goddess who founded the city of Athens chose to locate it in a country with a temperate climate that made men prudent, as the Egyptian priests taught Solon: "*The air at Athens is thin, and that is why the Athenians are considered more acute; at Thebes it is heavy, and thus Thebans are considered more thick-witted and stronger*,">>[267] <so that, just as fruits and animals grow differently, men too are born more or less bellicose, just, temperate, and docile:> <<here subject to wine, there to theft or to lewdness; here inclined to superstition, there to

266. Vegetius, I, ii, in Justus Lipsius, *Politicorum*, V, 10.
267. Cicero, *De fato*, IV.

unbelief; here to liberty, there to servitude;>> <capable of a science or an art, dull or ingenious, obedient or rebellious, good or bad, as the place where they are located inclines them. And, like trees, they take on a new complexion if they change their place. That was the reason Cyrus did not want to let the Persians abandon their harsh and cragged country and move to another that was mild and flat,> <<saying that rich and soft lands made men soft, and that fertile lands made minds infertile.>> <If by some celestial influence, we sometimes see one art, one opinion flourish and sometimes another, a particular century produce a particular nature and incline the human race in a particular direction; if we see the minds of men sometimes vigorous and sometimes unproductive, like our fields, what becomes of all those fine prerogatives on which we flatter ourselves? Since a wise man can be mistaken, and a hundred men, and a hundred nations, let alone that human nature, as we believe, is several centuries off in this or that, what assurance do we have that sometimes it stops being wrong> <<and that it is not wrong in this century?>>

It seems to me that, among other testimonies to our imbecility, this one deserves not to be forgotten, that even by desire man does not know how to find what he needs; even by imagination and wish, quite apart from enjoyment, we could not agree on what we need to satisfy us. Leave it to our thought to cut and sew at its pleasure, it cannot even desire what is fit for it <<and satisfy itself:>>

> <. . . for what do we fear or desire through reason?
> What do you conceive so dexterously
> That when carried through and finished you do not wish it
>   undone?>[268]

That is why <<Socrates did not ask anything of the gods but to give him what they thought was good for him. And the Lacedaemonians' prayer, both public and private, was simply that good and fair things be granted them, leaving their selection and choice to divine discretion:>>

> <We ask for wives and offspring, and they know
> Of what kind the future wife and children are.>[269]

And the Christian asks God that his will be done, in order not to fall into the difficulty that the poets invent for King Midas. He asked the

268. Juvenal, Satires, X, 4–6.
269. Juvenal, Satires, X, 352–3.

gods that everything he touched should be turned to gold. His prayer
was granted: his wine turned to gold, his bread turned to gold, and the
feather of his bed, and of gold was his shirt and his clothing, so that he
found himself overwhelmed under the enjoyment of his desire and bur-
dened with an insupportable benefit. He had to unpray his prayers,

> Astonished by the new evil, rich and poor,
> He wishes to flee his wealth, and hates what he had
>   desired.[270]

<Let us speak of my own case. When I was young, I asked from for-
tune, as much as anything else, the order of Saint Michael, for that was
then the highest mark of honor of the French nobility and very rare.
Fortune kindly granted it to me. Instead of mounting me and lifting me
from my place to attain it, she treated me much more graciously: she
degraded and lowered it to my shoulders and below.>
<<Cleobis and Biton, Trophonius and Agamedes, having asked, the
former their goddess, the latter their god, for a recompense worthy of
their piety, had death for a reward, so different from ours are celestial
opinions of what we need.>>
God could allow us riches, honors, life, and even health, sometimes
to our own hurt; for all that is pleasant for us is not always good for us. If
in place of healing, he sends us death or the worsening of our afflic-
tions—"Thy rod and thy staff have comforted me"—he does it for reasons of his providence, which considers what is due us with much
greater certainty than we can do, and we must take it in good part, as
from a most wise and most beneficent hand:

> <. . . if you want advice,
> Allow the gods themselves to decide
> What suits us and what is good for our concerns;
> Man is dearer to them than to himself.[271]

For to require of them honors and responsibilities is to require that they
cast you into a battle or subject you to a throw of the dice, or some other
thing of which the outcome is unknown to you and the fruit doubtful.>
There is no battle so violent among philosophers and so bitter as that
which turns on the question of the sovereign good for man, <<from
which, according to Varro, there sprang 288 sects.

270. Ovid, Metamorphoses, XI, 128–9.
271. Juvenal, Satires, X, 346–8.

"For he who disputes about the highest good is disputing about the whole of philosophy.">>[272]

> *Three guests appear to me to disagree,*
> *Whose different tastes lead to different foods.*
> *What to give them, what not to give them? You refuse*
> *What the other likes. What you seek is wholly hateful and*
> *bitter to the other two.*[273]

Nature should respond in this way to their contestations and their debates.

Some say our well-being resides in virtue, others in pleasure, others in consenting to nature; one, in knowledge; <<one, in being free of pain;>> another, in not letting ourselves be carried away by appearances (and that idea seems to be related to that other one <of old Pythagoras:>

> *To marvel at nothing is the one and only thing, Numacius,*
> *That can make and keep us happy,*[274]

which is the goal of the Pyrrhonian sect). <<Aristotle attributes the ability to marvel at nothing to magnanimity.>> And Arcesilaus said that constancy and rigidity and inflexibility of judgment were goods, but consent and application were vices and evils. It is true that insofar as he was establishing this by a certain axiom, he was departing from Pyrrhonism. The Pyrrhonians, when they say that the sovereign good is *ataraxia*, which is the immobility of the judgment, do not mean to say it in an affirmative fashion; but the same movement of their soul that makes them flee precipices and take shelter from the evening dew is what presents this idea to them and makes them reject any other.

<How I wish that while I live either someone else or Justus Lipsius, the most learned man who remains to us, of a most polished and judicious mind, truly akin to my Turnebus, had both the intent and the health and enough leisure to assemble in a list, according to their divisions and classes, sincerely and inquiringly, as far as we can see, the opinions of ancient philosophy on the subject of our being and our customs, their controversies, the standing and succession of sects, the application of the lives of the authors and partisans to their precepts in

272. Cicero, *De finibus*, V, v.
273. Horace, *Epistles*, II, ii, 61–4.
274. Horace, *Epistles*, I, vi, 1–2.

memorable and exemplary occasions. What a fine and useful work that would be!>

As for the rest, if it is from ourselves that we draw the regulation of our customs, into what confusion we throw ourselves! For what our reason advises us as most likely is generally that each person obey the laws of his country, <like the view of Socrates, inspired, he says, by divine counsel.> And what can be meant by this except that our duty has no rule but chance? Truth must have an identical and universal countenance. If man knew what gave body and true being to right and justice, he would not attach them to the condition of the customs of this or that country; it would not be through the fancy of the Persians or the Indians that virtue would take its form. There is nothing subject to more continual agitation than the laws. Since I was born, I have seen those of the English, our neighbors, change three or four times, not only on the subject of politics, which is the one that can be excused from constancy, but on the most important subject possible, that is, on the subject of religion. I am the more ashamed and troubled by this, since that is a nation with which those of my province once had such close connections that there are still in my house some traces of our former kinship.

<<And even among us I have seen what was a capital offense become legitimate; and in the same way as we ourselves think of others according to the uncertainty of the fortunes of war, we go from being one day guilty of lèse-majesté both human and divine, our justice falling to the mercy of injustice, to taking an opposite nature in the space of a few years' possession.

How could that ancient God more clearly accuse human knowledge of ignorance of the divine being and teach men that religion was only something they had invented, useful for binding their society, than by declaring, as he did to those who came for instruction to his tripod, that the true worship for everyone was the one he found in use in the place where he happened to be? Oh, God! What an obligation we have to the goodness of our sovereign creator for having enlightened our belief beyond those wandering and arbitrary devotions and seated it on the eternal foundation of his holy word!>>

What then will philosophy tell us in this necessity? That we should follow the laws of our country, that is to say, that floating sea of opinions of a people or of a prince, who paint justice for me in as many colors and will reshape it in as many aspects as it will have in itself changes of passion? I cannot have such flexible judgment. What virtue is it that I see approved today and not tomorrow <<and that crossing a river makes a crime?

What truth is it that is bounded by these mountains and that is falsehood in the world beyond them?>>

But they are amusing when, to give some certainty to the laws, they say there are some they call natural that are perpetual and immutable and imprinted in the human race by its very essence. And of these, some make the number three, some four, some more, some less: a sign that this is a kind as doubtful as the rest. Now they are so unfortunate — for what can I call it but misfortune, that of so infinite a number of laws there is not at least one that chance <<and the temerity of fate>> have permitted to be universally received by the consent of all nations? — they are, I say, so miserable that of those three or four laws chosen there is not a single one that is not contradicted and disavowed, not by one nation, but by several. Now the only likely sign by which they can argue for any natural laws is universality of approbation. For what nature had truly ordained for us we would doubtless follow with common consent. And not only every nation but every particular man would resent the force and violence done him by someone who would urge him to act against that law. But let them just show me one of this condition. Protagoras and Ariston give the justice of laws no other essence but the authority and opinion of the legislator, and they claim that, apart from that, goodness and honesty would lose their qualities and remain empty names of indifferent things. Thrasymachus, in Plato, holds that there is no other right than the advantage of the superior. There is nothing in which the world differs so much as in customs and laws. That thing is abominable here that carries approbation elsewhere, as in Lacedaemon dexterity in stealing. Marriages between close relatives are capital offenses with us; elsewhere they are honored:

> *. . . they speak of countries*
> *Where mother is united with son, daughter with father,*
> *And filial piety grows with love.*[275]

Infanticide, patricide, wives in common, traffic in robberies, license in all kinds of voluptuousness: in short there is nothing so extreme that it is not found to be accepted as the custom of some nation.

<It is credible that there are natural laws, as we see them in other creatures; but in us they are lost, that fair human reason insinuating itself everywhere to manage and command, mixing and confounding the face of things according to its vanity and inconstancy.> <<*Thus nothing remains that is really ours; what I call ours is the product of art.*>>[276]

275. Ovid, *Metamorphoses*, X, 331–3.
276. Cicero, *De finibus*, V, xxi.

Subjects have different lusters and different considerations; that is what chiefly produces the diversity of opinions. One nation looks at a subject from one aspect, another from another aspect.

There is nothing so horrible to imagine as eating one's father. The people who formerly acknowledged that custom nevertheless took it for a testimony of piety and genuine affection, seeking by this to give their progenitors the worthiest and most honorable sepulcher, lodging in themselves and in their marrow the bodies and the remains of their fathers, bringing them to life somehow and regenerating them by the transmutation into their living flesh through digestion and nourishment. It is easy to understand what cruelty and abomination it would have been to men steeped in and imbued with this superstition to throw their parents' remains to the corruption of the earth and the nourishment of beasts and worms.

Lycurgus considered in theft the vivacity, diligence, boldness, and dexterity involved in snatching something from your neighbor, and the benefit accruing to the public, in that each person thus looks more carefully to the conservation of what is his own, and he believed that from this double institution of assault and defense there would be more considerable lessons for military discipline (which was the principal science and virtue toward which he wished to guide that nation) than from the disorder and injustice of taking another's goods.

The tyrant Dionysius offered Plato a robe in the Persian fashion, long, damasked, and perfumed; Plato refused it, saying that being a man, he could not willingly dress in a woman's robe, but Aristippus accepted it, with this reply: that no garb could corrupt a chaste heart. <<His friends berated his cowardice for letting Dionysius spit in his face: "To catch a gudgeon," he said, "fishermen allow themselves to be soaked from head to foot by the waves of the sea." Diogenes was washing cabbages and, when he saw Aristippus passing, remarked, "If you knew how to live on cabbages, you would not pay court to a tyrant." To which Aristippus replied, "If you knew how to live among men, you would not wash cabbages.">> Thus reason furnishes likelihood for different cases. <It is a pot with two handles that can be grasped by the left or the right:

> . . . you threaten war, oh, earth whose guest I am;
> These horses are armed for war, these troops warn of war.
> Yet these same quadrupeds submit to the chariot
> And are joined in concordance to the same yoke.
> There is hope of peace.>[277]

277. Virgil, *Aeneid*, III, 539–43.

<<Solon was admonished not to shed impotent and useless tears for the death of his son. "That is why it is more justly that I shed them," he said, "because they are useless and impotent." Socrates' wife found her grief aggravated by this circumstance: "Oh, how unjustly those wicked judges make him die!" He replied to her: "Would you prefer that it be justly?">>

We have pierced ears; the Greeks thought this a mark of servitude. We retire in private to enjoy our women; the Indians do it in public. The Scythians immolated strangers in their temples; elsewhere temples serve as sanctuary.

<The vulgar have their fury because every country
Hates the gods of its neighbor and believes
That only those it worships are really gods.>[278]

I have heard a judge spoken of who, when he encountered a bitter conflict between Bartolus and Baldus, and some matter stirred up by many contradictions, wrote at the margin of his book: A *question for a friend*, in other words, that the truth was so tangled and disputed that in such a case he could favor whichever of the parties he pleased. It was only for lack of wit and competence that he could not put everywhere: A *question for a friend*. The lawyers and judges of our time find enough bias in all their cases to adjust them as they like. In a science so infinite, depending on the authority of so many opinions and on so arbitrary a subject, there cannot but arise an extreme confusion of judgments. Moreover, there is no trial at all so clear that there are not different views of it. What one group has decided, the other decides the opposite way, and they themselves go the opposite way another time. We see ordinary examples of this in the license that stains to a surprising degree the ceremonious and lustrous authority of our justice, not to let the decisions decide, and to run from some judges to others to decide on a given case.

As to the freedom of philosophical opinions touching vice and virtue, that is a matter we need not go into at length and where there are numerous opinions that are better kept silent than published <<to weak minds.>> <Arcesilaus said there was nothing in lewdness, from whatever side and wherever it was practiced.> <<"As to obscene desires, if nature demands them, neither race nor place nor rank is to be considered but only grace, age, and beauty, according to the view of Epicurus."[279]

278. Juvenal, *Satires*, XV, 37–9.
279. Cicero, *Tusculan Disputations*, V, xxxiii.

"Nor are sacred loves thought to be foreign to the wise man."[280] "We *should ask up to what age young men are to be loved."*[281] These two last Stoic sayings and, on that subject, the reproach of Dicaearchus to Plato himself, show how much the sanest philosophy suffers from excessive liberties far from common practice.>>

The laws receive their authority from possession and custom; it is dangerous to trace them back to their beginning; they grow great and become nobler as they run on, like our rivers; follow them backward to their source, there is only a little jet of water scarcely recognizable, which thus swells and fortifies itself when it grows old. Look at the ancient considerations that gave the first movement to this famous torrent, full of dignity, awe, and reverence: you will find them so light and delicate that it is no wonder the people here who weigh everything and reduce everything to reason, and receive nothing from authority and reputation, often have their judgments very far from public ones. It is no wonder if people who take for their patron the first image of nature should swerve from the common path in most of their opinions. For example, few among them would have approved of the constraining conditions of our marriages, <<and most of them have wanted wives in common and without obligation.>> They rejected our ceremonies. Chrysippus said a philosopher would do a dozen somersaults in public, and without his breeches, for a dozen olives. <<That philosopher would scarcely have advised Cleisthenes to refuse his daughter, the lovely Agarista, to Hippoclides, because he had seen him stand on his head on a table with his legs wide apart.

Metrocles rather indiscreetly farted while debating in the presence of his students, and kept to his house, hiding in shame, until Crites came to visit him. Adding to his consolations and arguments the example of his freedom, and setting out to fart in competition with him, he cured him of that scruple and, further, enlisted him in his own more easygoing Stoic sect, as against the more politely mannered Peripatetic sect, to which he had previously belonged.

What we call decency—not to dare do in public what we think it decent to do in private—the Stoics called stupidity; and to be so refined as to conceal and disavow what nature, custom, and our desire publish and proclaim of our actions, they considered a vice. To [the Peripatetics] it seemed it was disturbing the mysteries of Venus to remove them from the private sacristy of her temple so as to expose them to the view

280. Cicero, *De finibus*, III, xx.
281. Seneca, *Epistles*, CXXIII.

of the people; and to bring her games out from behind the curtain was to debase them. (Shame is a kind of weight; concealment, reservation, circumscription are parts of esteem.) They thought that under the mask of virtue, sensual pleasure very ingeniously made its case not to be prostituted in the city squares, trodden underfoot, and exposed to the public view, lacking the dignity and convenience of its usual chambers. Hence>> some say that to eliminate public brothels is not only to spread everywhere the lewdness that had been assigned to that place, but even to sting men to this vice by making it more inconvenient:

> Aufidia's husband, Corvinus, you become her lover
> When she is your rival's wife.
> Another's wife pleases you who, when yours, displeases you.
> Well! When secure are you impotent?[282]

This experience is diversified in a thousand examples:

> Cecilianus, no one in the whole city wanted to touch your wife
> Freely, when it was permitted. But now that you have her guarded,
> There is a great crowd of copulators. You are a clever husband.[283]

Someone asked a philosopher who was surprised in this activity what he was doing. He replied quite coldly: "I am planting a man," blushing no more at being so caught than if they had caught him planting garlic.

<<It is, as I believe, out of too tender and respectful a view that a great and religious author was so necessarily committed to privacy and shame that he could not persuade himself that, to maintain the impudence of their school's teaching, their activity had to reach its completion in the license of those cynical embraces, but stopped at the mere representation of lascivious movements; and afterward, to eject what shame had constrained and kept back, they had to withdraw into the shade. He had not looked far enough ahead in their debauches. For Diogenes, masturbating in public, expressed to those watching a wish that he could thus satisfy his stomach by rubbing it. To those who asked him why he did not look for somewhere more convenient to eat than in the open street, he replied, "Because I am hungry in the open street."

282. Martial, *Epigrams*, II, lii.
283. Martial, *Epigrams*, I, lxxiv.

The women philosophers who joined their sect also joined with their persons everywhere, without discretion. And Hipparchia was not received in the society of Crates except on the condition of following the practices and customs of its rule in everything. These philosophers set a great price on virtue and rejected all other disciplines but morality. Yet in all their actions they attributed the highest authority, above the law, to the decision of their sage, and they set no limit to sensual pleasure>> except moderation and the conservation of the liberty of others.

From the fact that wine seems bitter to the sick person and pleasant to the healthy one, that the rudder looks bent in the water and straight to those who see it out of the water, and other contrary appearances that are found in subjects, Heraclitus and Protagoras argued that all subjects had in them the causes of these appearances, and there was in the wine some bitterness that bore some relation to the sick man's taste, the rudder, some bent quality relating to the person who looks at it in the water. And so with all the rest. Which is to say that everything is in all things and consequently nothing in any one, for nothing is where everything is.

This opinion reminds me of the experience we have: that there is no sense or trait, whether straight or bitter or sweet or curved, that the human mind does not find in the writings it undertakes to excavate. How much falsehood and deception has not been brought forth in the cleanest, purest, and most perfect word possible? What heresy has not found sufficient foundation and sufficient testimony to establish and maintain itself? That is why the authors of such errors never want to depart from this proof, from the testimony of the interpretation of words. A person of dignity, who wanted to use authority to justify to me that search for the philosopher's stone in which he was deeply engaged, recently cited to me five or six passages from the Bible, which he said he had first relied on to satisfy his conscience (for he is a cleric); and, in truth, the device was not only pleasant but also very aptly suited to the defense of that fair science.

That is how the reputation of fables of divination is established. If we have the authority to leaf through and search curiously all the folds and glosses of his words, there is no prognosticator whom one cannot make say whatever one wants, like the sibyls; for there are so many ways of interpreting that it is hard to prevent an ingenious mind from finding in every subject, whether obliquely or directly, something that serves him to make his point.

<<Yet we find a nebulous and doubtful style in such frequent and ancient use! Let the author manage to attract and attach posterity to himself (which not only his competence but as much or more a chance

interest in the subject matter may bring about); for the rest, he presents himself, by stupidity or by cleverness, a bit obscurely and inconsistently—it makes no difference to him! A number of minds, sifting and shaking him, will squeeze out a quantity of ideas either according to his meaning, or at a tangent to, or against it, all of which will do him honor. He will see himself enriched through his disciples, like the regents of Lendit.>>

That is what has given value to many things worth nothing, has given reputation to many writings, and credited them with any sort of matter you like: the same thing receiving thousands of images and different considerations, as many as you wish. <<Is it possible that Homer wanted to say everything he has been made to say, and that he used as many and as varied figures as the theologians, legislators, captains, philosophers, every sort of people who treat sciences, as differently and contrarily as they treat them, attribute to him, and cite from him: general master of all offices, works, and artisans, general counselor for all enterprises?>> Whoever needs oracles or predictions has found them to his purpose. It is amazing how many occasions a learned person, and a friend of mine, draws out of Homer in favor of our religion, and he cannot easily be dissuaded of the opinion that that was Homer's aim (yet he is as familiar with that author as with a man of our time.) <<And what he finds in favor of our time, others had formerly found in favor of theirs.

See how Plato is tossed about and debated. Everyone, applying Plato to himself in his own honor, puts him down on whatever side he wants. He is drawn in and inserted into all the new opinions that the world accepts, and is made to disagree with himself according to the different course of things. They make him disavow, according to his own meaning, the customs permissible in his century, insofar as they are impermissible in ours. All this is done with liveliness and power, to the extent that the mind of the interpreter is powerful and lively.>>

From the same foundation as that of Heraclitus and his proposition that all things had in them the features we discern, Democritus drew quite the opposite conclusion: that these subjects had nothing at all of what we find there. And from the fact that honey was sweet to one and bitter to another he argued that it was neither bitter nor sweet. The Pyrrhonians said they did not know if it is sweet or bitter, or neither the one nor the other, or both; for they always reached the high point of doubtfulness.

<<The Cyrenaics held that nothing is perceptible outside us, and that what was perceptible was only what touched us inwardly, like pain and pleasure, acknowledging neither sound nor color, but only certain

affections that come to us from them; they held that man has no other basis for his judgment. Protagoras thought that what seems to each person to be true was true for him. The Epicureans locate all judgment in sense both in their account of things and in pleasure. Plato wanted the judgment of truth, and truth itself, separated from opinions and from the senses, to belong to mind and to cogitation.>>

[7. The Senses Are Inadequate]

This discussion has brought me to the consideration of the senses, in which we find the greatest foundation and proof of our ignorance. Whatever is known is doubtless known by the faculty of the knower. For since judgment comes from the activity of the person judging, it is logical that he performs this act by his own powers and his own will, not through the constraint of another, as would be the case if we knew things by the power of their essence and according to its law. But all knowledge is conveyed to us by the senses: they are our masters:

> < . . . for by this way the paved path of belief
> Leads straightest into the heart of man and the temples of his
> mind.>[284]

Knowledge begins through them and is resolved into them. After all, we would know no more than a stone if we did not know that there is sound, smell, light, taste, measure, weight, softness, hardness, sharpness, color, smoothness, size, and depth. Here is the platform and principle of the whole structure of our knowledge. <<And, according to some, knowledge is nothing else but sensation.>> He who could push me into contradicting the senses would have me by the throat; he could not push me further back. The senses are the beginning and the end of human knowledge:

> You will find that the idea of truth is derived first from the
> senses
> And that the senses cannot be challenged . . .
> What should be thought more certain than sense?[285]

Let them be credited with as little as possible, they will always have to be granted this: that all our instruction is routed by their means and

284. Lucretius, De rerum natura, V, 103.
285. Lucretius, De rerum natura, IV, 478, 482.

mediation. Cicero says that Chrysippus, when he wanted to attack the power and virtue of the senses, represented to himself so many arguments to the contrary and such vehement oppositions that he could not satisfy himself with them. On this Carneades, who supported the opposite side, boasted that he could use the very arms and words of Chrysippus to combat him and in this connection wrote against him: "O wretched one, your power has destroyed you!" There can be nothing more absurd in our view than to maintain that fire does not heat, that light does not illuminate, that there is no weight or solidity in iron—all of which are things conveyed to us by the senses. Nor is there belief or knowledge in man that can be compared in certainty with this.

The first consideration I have on the subject of the senses is that I doubt that man is provided with all the natural senses. I see a number of animals that live a complete and perfect life, some without sight, others without hearing. Who knows if one, two, three, or more other senses are lacking in us also? For if some sense is lacking, our reasoning cannot discover the defect. It is the privilege of the senses to be the extreme limit of our awareness; there is nothing beyond them that can help us discover them, no more than one sense can discover another,

> <Or will the ears be able to reprove the eyes,
> Or touch, the ears? Or will the taste in the mouth
> Refute this touch; will the nostrils disprove it
> Or the eyes prove it false?>[286]

They all establish the extreme limit of our abilities,

> . . . for each sense has its power divided,
> Each its own force.[287]

It is impossible to make a man blind by nature understand that he does not see, impossible to make him want sight and regret his lack.

For this reason we should not take any confidence from the fact that our soul is contented and satisfied with what we have, given that it has no way of knowing its illness and its imperfection in this, if there is one. It is impossible to say anything to that blind man, by reasoning, argument, or analogy, that accommodates in his imagination any apprehension of light, color, and vision. There is nothing further that can make the sense evident. As to those who are born blind, whom we find wanting to see, it

286. Lucretius, De rerum natura, IV, 487–9.
287. Lucretius, De rerum natura, IV, 490–1.

is not that they understand what they are asking for. They have heard from us that there is something they should say, that there is something for them to desire that we have, <<something they can easily name, as well as its effects and consequences;>> but still they do not know what that is, nor do they grasp it from either near or far.

I saw a gentleman of good family, born blind, or at least blind from an age such that he did not know what vision is; he understands so little what he lacks, that he uses and employs words proper to vision as we do and applies them in a way that is entirely his own and idiosyncratic. He was presented with a child to whom he was godfather. Taking it in his arms he said: "Oh, lord! What a lovely child! How beautiful it looks! What a pretty face it has!" He will say, like one of us, "This room has a fine view; the weather is good; there is bright sunshine." There is more: since hunting, tennis, and shooting are our sports, and he has heard this said, he takes a liking to them, and busies himself with them, and believes he has the same part in them that we do; he is annoyed and pleased by them, and yet he knows about them only through the ears. Someone calls out to him, "There's a hare!" when he is on some plain where he can use his spurs; and again someone says to him "There's a hare caught!" and there he is, as proud of his prize as he has heard others say they are. He takes a tennis ball in his left hand and hits it with his racket; he shoots with his musket at random, and is satisfied when his people tell him he is too high or at the side.

How do we know if the human race makes a similar stupid mistake about some sense and most of the appearance of things is hidden from us through this defect? How do we know if the difficulties we find in numerous works of nature come from this? And if numerous achievements of animals that exceed our capacity are produced by the power of some sense that we lack? And if by this means some of them have a life more full and complete than ours? We grasp the apple as it were with all our senses; we find in it redness, smoothness, odor, and sweetness; beyond that, it may have other virtues, like drying up or shrinking, for which we have no sense to inform us. As to the properties we call occult in a number of things, like the magnet's ability to attract iron, is it not likely that there are sensitive capacities in nature fit for judging and perceiving them and that the lack of such capacities produces our ignorance of the true essence of such things? It is perhaps some particular sense that lets cocks know the hour of morning and of midnight and moves them to crow; <<that teaches chickens, before any practice or experience, to fear a sparrow hawk and not a goose or a peacock, which are large birds; that cautions hens against the hostile attitude a cat has to them and tells them not to fear a dog: to arm them against the meowing,

somehow flattering, voice, but not against the barking, harsh, and quarrelsome voice; that teaches wasps, ants, and rats always to choose the best cheese and the best pear before they have tasted it,>> and that has led the deer, <<the elephant, the snake>> to the recognition of a certain herb able to cure them. There is no sense that does not have a broad dominion and that does not produce by its means infinite items of knowledge. If we lacked the understanding of sounds, of harmony, and of the voice, that would bring unimaginable confusion to all the rest of our knowledge. For besides what is attached to the proper activity of each sense, how many arguments, inferences, and conclusions do we make to other things through the comparison of one sense with another! Let an intelligent man imagine human nature originally produced without sight, and consider how much ignorance and trouble such a defect would bring him, how much darkness and blindness in our soul. From this we will see how much the privation of another such sense would bear on the knowledge of the truth, let alone of two or three, if there is such knowledge in us. We have fashioned a truth through the consultation and concurrence of our five senses; but perhaps it would need the accord of eight or ten senses and their contribution to apprehend the truth certainly and in its essence.

The sects that oppose man's knowledge do so chiefly through the uncertainty and weakness of our senses: for since our knowledge comes to us through and by means of them, if they fail in the report they give us, if they corrupt and alter what they bring us from outside, if the light that flows into the soul is obscured in its passage, we have nothing else to hold on to. From this extreme difficulty arise all those ideas: that every subject has in itself everything we find in it; that it has nothing of what we think we find in it; and that the sun is no larger than it looks to us, as the Epicureans contend.

> <Whatever it is, is of no greater shape
> Than it seems to be as we see it with our eyes;>[288]

that the appearances that present a body as large to a person near to it, and smaller to one who is farther away, are both true,

> <Nor do we conclude from this that the eyes are deceptive
> Or charge to them the errors of the mind,>[289]

288. Lucretius, *De rerum natura*, V, 577.
289. Lucretius, *De rerum natura*, IV, 380, 387.

and, resolutely, that there is no deceit in the senses; that we must lie at
their mercy and seek elsewhere for reasons to excuse the diversity and
contradiction we find in them, going so far as to invent any other lie and
fancy (they go that far) rather than to accuse the senses. <<Timagoras
swore that by pressing or turning his eye he had never seen the light of
the candle doubled and that this appearance came from the vice of
opinion, not from the instrument.>> Of all absurdities the most absurd,
<<for the Epicureans,>> is to disavow the force and efficacy of the senses:

> *Whatever has been seen at some time is true.*
> *And if reason cannot distinguish the cause*
> *Why those things that seen near at hand were square*
> *Are seen round at a distance, still it is better*
> *Through lack of argument to err in accounting*
> *For the causes of either shape*
> *Rather than to allow things clearly seen to elude your grasp,*
> *Attack the grounds of belief, and tear up the foundations*
> *On which life and existence rest.*
> *For not only would all reasoning collapse,*
> *But so, straight away, would life itself,*
> *Unless we choose to trust the senses,*
> *And avoid precipitous places*
> *And other things of the kind that are to be shunned.*[290]

<<This desperate advice, so unphilosophical, represents nothing if
not that human knowledge can maintain itself only by unreasonable,
foolish, mad reasoning; but it is still better for man to put a higher value
on himself by using any other remedy, however fantastic it may be,
than to confess his ineluctable stupidity—a truth so disadvantageous to
him! He cannot avoid the fact that the senses are the sovereign masters
of his knowledge, but they are uncertain and falsifiable in all circumstances. It is there that we have to fight it out to the last, and if we lack
the appropriate powers, as we do, to use at this juncture obstinacy,
temerity, and impudence.>>

    <In case what the Epicureans say is true, that we have no knowledge
if the appearances of the senses are false, and what the Stoics say—that
it is also true that the appearances of the senses are so false that they can
produce no knowledge—we shall conclude, at the expense of these two
great dogmatic sects, that there is no knowledge.>

290. Lucretius, *De rerum natura*, IV, 500–11.

As to the error and uncertainty of the operation of the senses, everyone can furnish as many examples as he likes, so commonplace are the faults and deceptions they impose on us. In the echo of a valley, the sound of a trumpet coming from behind us seems to come from in front:

<Mountains seen far off in the waters
Seem to be united in a single mass . . .
The hills and plains seem to be moving toward the stern,
When it is our vessel that is driving along . . .
If our horse stops in midstream,
We think it is carried by a countercurrent.>[291]

If you take a musket ball under the forefinger, with the middle finger lapped around it, you have to push yourself very hard indeed to admit that there is only one, so strongly do the senses represent them to us as two. For it is frequently seen that our senses are masters of our reasoning and compel it to receive impressions that it knows and judges to be false. I set aside the sense of touch, which has its operations so close by, so lively and substantial, and which, through the effect of the pain that it brings to the body, so often overturns all those fine Stoic resolutions and compels to shout at his belly the person who has with all resolution established in his soul the dogma that colic, like every other disease and pain, is an indifferent matter, having no power to lessen in any way the sovereign happiness and felicity in which the sage is housed through his virtue. There is no heart so soft that the sound of our drums and trumpets does not warm it, nor so hard that the sweetness of music does not arouse and tickle it; and no soul so harsh that it does not find itself touched with some reverence in considering that somber vastness of our churches, the diversity of ornaments and order of our ceremonies and hearing the devout sound of our organs and the solemn and religious harmony of our voices. Even those who enter with distrust feel some shiver in their heart and some dread that makes them question their opinion.

<As for me, I do not believe myself strong enough to listen sedately to verses of Horace or Catullus sung in a competent voice by a fair young mouth.>

<<And Zeno was right to say that the voice was the flower of beauty. Someone once wanted to make me believe that a man known to all Frenchmen had impressed me when reciting some verses he had composed, which were not the same on paper as in the air, and that my eyes

291. Lucretius, De rerum natura, IV, 397–8, 389–90, 420–1.

were making a judgment contrary to my ears, so great a power has pronunciation to give value and style to works that are left to its sway. In this connection Philoxenus was not much to blame when, hearing someone give a bad tone to some composition of his, he started to kick and break some earthenware belonging to that person, saying, "I am breaking what is yours, as you are corrupting what is mine.">>

For what purpose did those very people who had committed themselves to dying with a certain resolution turn away their face so as not to see the blow they had asked to be given? And why cannot those who for their own health desire and order that they be cut and cauterized endure the sight of the preparations, tools, and operations of the surgeon—given that the sight has no share in the pain? Are not these good examples to verify the authority that the senses have for our reasoning? It is no use knowing that these tresses are borrowed from a page or a lackey, that this rouge came from Spain, and this whitening and polish from the ocean; it still happens that vision forces us to find the subject more loveable and more agreeable, against all reason. For in this there is nothing of its own.

> We are won over by clothes; our judgments are deceived
> By gold and jewels; the girl's least part is her own.
> Often you seek what you love among so many:
> Rich love deceives those eyes with its shield.[292]

How much the poets grant to the power of the senses when they make Narcissus lost in the love of his shadow:

> In all that is admired he himself is admirable;
> Imprudently he desires himself; and he who praises is himself
>   praised,
> And while seeking is sought; and at the same time he both
>   kindles and burns,[293]

and Pygmalion's understanding so troubled by the impression of the sight of his ivory statue, which he loves and treats as if it were alive:

> He gives kisses, and believes they are returned;
> He follows and holds and believes the flesh

292. Ovid, *Remedia amoris*, 343–6.
293. Ovid, *Metamorphoses*, III, 424–6.

Gives way to his touching fingers
And fears a bruise may come to the pressed joints.[294]

Put a philosopher in a cage of small bars of thin iron suspended at the top of the towers of Notre Dame de Paris, he will see for obvious reasons that it is impossible for him to fall, and yet (unless he is used to the roofer's trade) he will not be able to keep the vision of that height from frightening and astonishing him. For we have enough trouble reassuring ourselves in the galleries of our steeples if they are made with open work, even though they are built of stone. There are some who cannot even bear the thought of it. Set a plank between those two towers, of a size such as is needed for us to walk on it: there is no philosophical wisdom of such firmness as to give us the courage to walk on it as we would do if it was on the ground. I have often found in our mountains here — although I am one of those who are only moderately afraid of such things — that I could not bear the sight of that infinite depth without horror and trembling of legs and thighs, even though I was more than my length from the edge and could not have fallen unless I had intended to expose myself to danger. I also noticed there that, whatever the height, if there was some tree in this incline or some rock jutting out to support our view a little and divide it, this alleviates our fear and gives us assurance, as if there were something from which we could get help in falling; but we cannot face sharp and undivided precipices without turning our head away: <<*"so that we cannot look down without dizziness of both eyes and mind,"*>>[295] which is an obvious deception of our sight. That fine philosopher put out his eyes to free his soul from the distractions he received from them, so that he could philosophize with greater freedom.

But on this account he would have to have his ears stopped up as well, <which Theophrastus says are the most dangerous instrument we have for receiving violent impressions to trouble and change us,> and in the end deprive himself of all the other senses, that is, of his being and his life. For they all have that power to command our reasoning and our soul. <<*"For often in some way minds are moved by the solemnity of voices and songs; often also by concern and fear."*>>[296] Physicians hold that certain dispositions are agitated to the point of fury by some sounds and instruments. I have seen people who could not bear to hear a bone gnawed under their table without losing patience, and there is hardly a

294. Ovid, *Metamorphoses*, X, 256–8.
295. Livy, *Histories*, XLVII, vi.
296. Cicero, *De divinatione*, I, xxxvii.

man who is not disturbed by that sharp and piercing noise that files make grating on iron. In the same way some people are moved to anger and hatred at hearing someone chewing near them or hearing someone speak who has his throat or nose blocked. Of what use was the flautist who coached Gracchus, softening, hardening, and shaping his master's voice when he was haranguing at Rome, if the movement and quality of the sound did not have the power to affect and alter the judgment of the hearers? Seriously, it's well to make such a fuss about the firmness of this fine faculty, which submits to being handled and changed by the shifts and alterations of so slight a breeze!

The same trick that the senses play on our understanding they in their turn have played on them. Our soul sometimes takes its own revenge: <<they lie and deceive one another as much as you like.>> What we see and hear when agitated by anger we do not see as it is:

There appear a twin sun and two cities of Thebes.[297]

The object we love seems to us more beautiful than it is,

<*And so we see those in many ways deformed and ugly
Dearly loved, even prospering in high favor*>[298]

and uglier the one we dislike. To a man who is bored and afflicted, the light of day seems overcast and cloudy. Our senses are not only altered, but often stupefied by the passions of the soul. How many things do we see that we take no notice of if our mind is otherwise occupied?

*Even in things plain to see you can notice,
If you are not paying attention, it is as if things
Were cut off from you all the time, and very far away.*[299]

It seems the soul retreats into itself and smiles at the powers of the senses. And so both the inside and the outside of man are full of weakness and falsehood.

<Those who have likened our life to a dream were right, perhaps more so than they thought. When we are dreaming, our soul lives, acts, exercises all its faculties, no more nor less than when it is awake, though more softly and obscurely, still not with so certain a difference as

---

297. Virgil, *Aeneid*, IV, 470.
298. Lucretius, *De rerum natura*, IV, 1152–3.
299. Lucretius, *De rerum natura*, IV, 808–11.

between night and bright daylight, but like night and shade: there it is asleep, here it slumbers, more or less. There is always darkness and Cimmerian darkness.>

<<We are awake while asleep and sleeping while awake. I do not see so clearly in sleep; but as to the waking state, I never find it wholly pure and without clouds. Even sleep when it is deep sometimes puts dreams to sleep. But our waking state is never so wide awake that it purges and dissipates altogether the reveries that are waking dreams and even worse than dreams.

Since our reason and our soul receive the fancies and opinions that arise in them while we are sleeping, and authorize the actions of our dreams with the same approval they give to those of the day, why do we not wonder whether our thought, our action, is not another state of dreaming and our waking some kind of sleep?>>

If the senses are our first judges, it is not only our own senses that must be called to counsel, for in regard to this faculty animals have as much of a claim as we do or even more. It is certain that some have more acute hearing than man, others sight, others feeling, others touch and taste. Democritus said that gods and beasts have sensitive faculties much more perfect than man. Our saliva cleans and dries our wounds; it kills the snake:

> And in these things there is a difference and disagreement
> So great that what is food to one is to the other biting poison.
> Often indeed a snake, touched by human saliva,
> Dies, and puts an end to itself by gnawing its own body.[300]

What quality do we assign to the saliva? According to us, or according to the snake? By which of the two senses shall we verify the true essence of it that we are seeking? Pliny says that in the Indies there are certain sea hares that are poison to us and we to them, so that we kill them simply by our touch: which is truly poison, the man or the fish? Which shall we believe, the fish of the man or the man of the fish? <One quality of the air infects a man but does not harm a steer; some other infects the steer, but does not harm the man. Which of the two will be the pestilent quality in truth and in nature?> Those who have jaundice see all things yellowish and paler than we do:

> <Everything looks yellow to the jaundiced.>[301]

300. Lucretius, *De rerum natura*, IV, 638–41.
301. Lucretius, *De rerum natura*, IV, 330.

Those who have the disease that physicians call *hyposphragma*, which is a suffusion of blood under the skin, see everything red and bloody. How do we know if these humors that change in this way the operation of our vision predominate in beasts and for them are ordinary? For we see some whose eyes are yellow like our sufferers from jaundice and others who have eyes that are bloody red; it is probable that to them the color of objects looks different from what it does to us; which of the two judgments will be the true one? For it is not said that the essence of things relates to man alone. Hardness, whiteness, depth, and sharpness pertain to the needs and knowledge of animals as they do to ours; nature has given the use of them to animals as it has to us. When we press on the eye, we perceive the bodies we are looking at as longer and more extended; a number of animals have their eyes pressed down in this way, so this length is presumably the real form of this body, not the one that our eyes give it in their ordinary position. <If we squeeze the eye from below, things look double to us:

> *Double the lights of the lamps with their flowery flames . . .*
> *Twofold the faces of men, and their bodies double.*>[302]

If we have our ears somehow impeded or the passage for hearing stopped, we receive the sound in an unusual fashion; animals that have their ears hairy, or have only a little hole instead of an ear, consequently do not hear what we hear and receive the sound differently. At festivals and theaters we see that when a painted sheet of glass of a certain color is set in front of the torches, everything in that place looks to us either green or yellow or violet:

> <*And this is often done with yellow and red and steely blue*
> *Awnings, when they flap and flutter, stretched over great*
>   *theaters,*
> *Spread everywhere on masts and beams.*
> *For there they tinge the assembly in the rows beneath,*
> *And infuse the splendor of the stage, of fathers and mothers*
>   *and gods,*
> *And make them flutter in their colors.*>[303]

It is likely that the eyes of animals, which we see are of a different color, produce for them appearances of bodies corresponding to their eyes.

302. Lucretius, *De rerum natura*, IV, 451, 453.
303. Lucretius, *De rerum natura*, IV, 73–8.

To judge the action of the senses we would first have to be in agreement with the animals, and secondly, among ourselves. That is what we decidedly are not; and we enter into debate all the time about the fact that we hear, see, or taste something differently from someone else, and we debate about the diversity of images the senses bring us as much as we do about anything. By the ordinary rule of nature, a child hears and sees differently from a man of thirty years, and he in turn hears and sees differently from a man in his sixties. For some the senses are more obscure and darker, for others, more open and sharper. We receive things differently according to what we are and to how they appear to us. Now since what appears to us is so uncertain and controversial, it is no longer a miracle if we are told that we can affirm that snow looks white to us, but that to establish if it is such in its essence and in truth is more than we are able to resolve; and with this beginning shaken, all knowledge of the world must necessarily go to rack and ruin. What about our senses themselves contradicting one another? To the sight a painting seems embossed; when handled it seems flat. Shall we say that musk, which smells good and tastes bad, is agreeable or not? There are herbs and unguents, proper for one part of the body, which injure another part; honey is pleasant to the taste, unpleasant to the sight. Take those rings cut out in the form of feathers, called "endless feathers": no eye can distinguish their size, or defend itself from the illusion that they grow larger on one side and contract on the other, coming to a point even while they are being rolled around the finger, although when you feel them they seem to you equal in size and entirely similar.

<As for those persons who, to aid their lust, in times past used magnifying glasses so that the members they were to use would please them more through that ocular enlargement: to which of their two senses did they give the prize, to vision, which represented their members as large and great as they liked, or to touch, which presented them as small and contemptible?>

Is it our senses that lend the subject these different conditions while the subjects nevertheless have only one? That is what we see in the bread we eat; it is only bread, but our use makes of it bones, blood, flesh, hair, and nails,

<As food, when it is distributed to all the limbs and members,
Perishes, and furnishes out of itself a new nature.>[304]

304. Lucretius, De rerum natura, III, 702–3.

The moisture sucked up by the root of a tree becomes trunk, leaf, and fruit; and the air, though itself but one, is made by the application of a trumpet into a thousand different sorts of sounds. Is it, I say, our senses that fashion these subjects into so many different qualities, or do they have them in themselves? And given this doubt, what can we determine of their true essence? Further, when the accidents of illness, of daydreaming, or of sleep make things appear to us differently from the way they appear to the healthy, the wise, and those who are awake, is it not likely that our normal condition and our natural humors also have something to give a being to things relating to their condition and to accommodate them to themselves, as our disordered humors do? And is not our health just as capable of giving them their appearance as illness is? <<Why does not the temperate as well as the intemperate person have a certain form of objects relative to it, and why will not it, too, imprint its character on them?

The sick person attributes to the wine flatness; the healthy person, flavor; the thirsty person, sheer delight.>>

Now since our condition accommodates things to itself and transforms them according to itself, we no longer know what things are in truth, for nothing comes to us except as falsified and altered by our senses. Where the compass, the square, and the rule are crooked, all the proportions derived from them and all buildings erected by their measure are also necessarily defective and failing. The uncertainty of our senses makes uncertain all that they produce:

> *Again, as in a building, if the first rule is astray*
> *And the square is wrong and falls out of the straight lines*
> *And the level sags a bit anywhere,*
> *The whole structure will necessarily be made faulty and*
>   *crooked,*
> *All awry, bulging, leaning forward or backward,*
> *Out of harmony, so that some parts already seem to want to*
>   *fall,*
> *Or do fall, all betrayed by the first wrong measurements;*
> *Just so must your reasoning about things be mistaken and*
>   *false,*
> *Which all springs from false senses.*[305]

For the rest, who can be fit to judge of these differences? As we say of debates about religion—that we need a judge who is not attached to

---

305. Lucretius, *De rerum natura*, IV, 414–21.

one or the other side, exempt from choice or affection, which is not possible among Christians—so it is likewise in this case. For if he is old, he cannot judge of the feeling of old age, being himself a party to the debate; the same if he is young, the same if healthy, the same if ill, sleeping, and waking. It would take someone exempt from all these qualities, so that, without preoccupation in his judgment, he would judge of these propositions as indifferent to him, and for this reason we would need a judge who never was.

To judge appearances that we receive from subjects, we would need a judicatory instrument; to verify that instrument, we would need demonstration; to verify the demonstration, an instrument; here we are going round a circle. Since the senses cannot stop our dispute, being themselves full of uncertainty, it must be up to reason; no reason can be established without another reason: here we are regressing to infinity. Our imagination does not apply itself to foreign objects, but is formed through the mediation of the senses; and the senses do not understand a foreign object, but only their own passions; and thus what we imagine and what appears to us are not from the object, but only from the passion and suffering of the senses, which passion and which object are different things; thus he who judges by appearances judges by something other than the object. And if you say that the passions of the senses convey to the soul, by resemblance, the quality of the foreign objects, how can the soul and the understanding assure themselves of this resemblance, since they have in themselves no commerce with the foreign objects? Just as someone who did not know Socrates could not say that his portrait resembles him. Now if nevertheless someone wanted to judge by appearances, if by all of them, that is impossible, for they interfere with one another by their contrarieties and discrepancies, as we see by experience. Will it be the case that certain chosen appearances govern the others? That choice would have to be verified by another choice, the second by a third, and so this will never be accomplished.

[8. Changing Man Cannot Know Changing or Unchanging Things]

Finally, there is no constant existence, neither of our being nor of that of objects. Both we and our judgment and all things mortal go on flowing and rolling endlessly. Thus nothing can be established for certain of the one or the other, both the judging and the judged being in a constant state of change and motion.

We have no communication with being, since all human nature is always in the middle between being born and dying, giving only an obscure appearance and shadow of itself, and an uncertain and weak opinion of itself.[306] And if by chance you fix your thought on wanting to grasp your being, that is no more nor less than if you wanted to take hold of water, for the more you squeeze and press what is by nature flowing everywhere, the more you lose what you wanted to seize and take hold of. Thus since all things are subject to passing from one change to another, reason, seeking a real subsistence there, finds itself disappointed, not being able to apprehend anything subsistent and permanent, since everything is either coming into being and is not yet at all or beginning to die before it is born. Plato said that bodies never had existence but only birth, <<thinking that Homer had made the ocean father of the gods, and Thetis their mother, to show us that all things are in perpetual flux, motion, and variation: an opinion common to all the philosophers before his time, as he says, except only for Parmenides, who refused motion to things, attaching great value to the power of that idea.>> Pythagoras said that all matter is flowing and labile; the Stoics, that there is no present time, and that what we call present is only the joining and coupling together of the future and the past; Heraclitus, that no man has ever entered twice into the same river; <Epicharmus, that he who has long since borrowed money does not owe it now and that he who was invited overnight to come to dinner turns out today not to be invited, given that it is no longer the same people: they have become others;> and that no mortal substance can be found twice in the same state, for through the suddenness and quickness of change, as soon as it dissipates, so soon does it reassemble; it comes and then it goes in such a way that what begins to be born never arrives at the perfection of being, inasmuch as birth is never completed and never stops as being at its end, but from the seed is always changing and being altered from one thing to another. Thus from human seed there is made in the mother's womb a fruit without form, then a formed infant, then, leaving the womb, a sucking infant. Then it becomes a boy, next a youth, then a mature man, then a man, and finally a decrepit aged man: so that age and subsequent generation always go on destroying and spoiling what went before,

> <For time changes the nature of the whole world;
> One state after another must overtake all things,
> Nor does anything remain like itself; all things migrate,
> Nature alters all things and forces them to turn.>[307]

306. What follows, to the penultimate paragraph of the *Apology*, is Montaigne's paraphrase of Amyot's translation of Plutarch, *Que signifiait ce mot: ei?*
307. Lucretius, *De rerum natura*, V, 826–9.

And then we stupidly fear one kind of death, while we have already passed and are passing so many others. For not only, as Heraclitus said, is the death of fire the generation of air and the death of air the generation of water, but we can see this even more plainly in ourselves. The flowering of the prime of life passes when old age arrives, and youth is finished in the flowering of the mature man, childhood in youth, and the first period dies in childhood, and yesterday dies in today, and today will die in tomorrow; and there is nothing that stays and is always one. For if it is thus, if we always remain the same and one, how is it that we enjoy now one thing and now another? How is it that we love and hate, praise and condemn, contrary things? How do we have different affections, no longer retaining the same sentiment within the same thought? For it is not likely that we would take on different passions without changing; and what suffers change does not remain one and the same, and if it is not one and the same, then it also is not. But as to being a complete being, that also changes being simply, constantly becoming another from another. And consequently the senses deceive us and lie to us by nature, taking what appears for what is for lack of knowing what it is that is. But what is it, then, that truly is? What is eternal, that is, what has never been born, will never have an end; time never brings it any change. For time is a mobile thing, which appears as in shadow, with matter always running and flowing without ever remaining stable or permanent. Anything to which the words "before and after," "has been and will be," are applied shows on the face of it that it is not a thing that is. For it would be great stupidity and a very obvious falsehood to say that that thing is which is not yet in being or has already ceased to be. As to the words "present," "instant," "now," by which it seems we chiefly support and found our awareness of time, when reason discovers it, it destroys everything on the spot, for it immediately splits and divides it into future and past as if it wanted necessarily to see it cut in two. The same thing happens to the nature that is being measured as to the time that measures it. For there is nothing there either that remains or that is subsistent, but all things there are are born, or being born, or dying. Thus it would be a sin to say of God, who alone is, that he was or will be. For these are terms of variation, passage, or vicissitude concerning things that cannot last or remain in being. Hence we must conclude that only God is, not in the least according to some measure of time, but according to an immutable and immobile eternity, not measured by time, nor subject to any variation, before which nothing is, nor will be afterward, nor newer or more recent, but one really real being, who with one single now fills always; and there is nothing that is truly real but him alone, without one's being able to say: He has been or he will be without beginning and without end.

To this so religious conclusion of a pagan, I wish only to join this testimony of the same kind as the end of this long and tedious discourse, which would afford me matter without end: "Oh, what a vile and abject thing," he says, "is man, if he does not raise himself above humanity!"[308] There you have a good word and a useful desire, but similarly absurd. For to make the hilt bigger than the hand, the armful bigger than the arm, and to hope to stride further than our legs can reach, is impossible and monstrous. Nor can man raise himself above himself and humanity, for he cannot see but with his eyes nor grasp except with his grip. He will raise himself if God extraordinarily gives him his hand; he will raise himself, abandoning and renouncing his own means, and letting himself be lifted and sustained by purely celestial ones.

<<It is for our Christian faith, and not for his Stoic virtue, to aspire to that divine and miraculous metamorphosis.>>

---

308. Seneca, *Quaestiones naturales*, I, Preface.